SO-AEI-869

America's Abraham Lincoln

AMERICAN
CAVALCADE

America's Abraham Lincoln

MAY McNEER

MARSHALL CAVENDISH
CORPORATION

GREY CASTLE PRESS

Published by Grey Castle Press, Lakeville, Connecticut.

Marshall Cavendish Edition, North Bellmore, New York.

Published in large print by arrangement with Houghton Mifflin Co.

Printed in the USA.

Library of Congress Cataloging-in-Publication Data

McNeer, May.
    America's Abraham Lincoln / by May McNeer.
       p.   cm.— (American cavalcade)
    Reprint. Originally published : Boston : Houghton Mifflin, 1957.
    Includes bibliographical references and index.
    Summary: A biography of the president who led the country through the stormy years of the Civil War.
    ISBN 1-55905-090-X (lg. print)
    1. Lincoln, Abraham, 1809–1865—Juvenile literature. 2. Presidents—United States—Biography—Juvenile literature. 3. Large type books. [1. Lincoln, Abraham, 1809–1865. 2. Presidents. 3. Large type books.] I. Title. II. Series.
[E457.905'M25 1991]
973.7'092—dc20
[B]
[92]   90-48982
                                            CIP
                                            AC

201098

ISBN 1-55905-090-X
     1-55905-100-0 (set)

Photo Credits:

Cover: Library of Congress
Library of Congress—pgs. 8, 53, 61, 66, 73, 85, 104, 116
Illinois State Historical Library—pgs. 18 (right), 77, 111
The Lincoln Museum, Fort Wayne, Indiana, a part of Lincoln National Corporation—pg. 18 (left)
The Bettmann Archive—pg. 120
U.S. Department of the Interior, National Park Service—pg. 122

040852

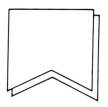

WILDERNESS TREES stood thick along the rough roads of Kentucky in 1816. In the pale dawn of an October day stars winked out of sight as two small children walking in the ruts of wagon wheels glanced back at the sight of fire flicker through a cabin door. Then they turned their faces toward Muldraugh's Hill, where Knob Creek rushed over the stones.

The boy was called Abraham, and he walked to school with his sister Sarah. Although he was tall, thin, and big-boned for a seven-year-old, he wore nothing but a homespun shirt that came down below his knees, for he was still young enough to be just a "shirttail boy."

"Come along, Abe. Hurry!"

"I'm a-coming, Sally."

Abe walked slowly, looking down at his shirt and shivering in the wind as his bare brown feet followed the wagon tracks. Then he smiled at the remembrance of his father's promise to give the skin of the next deer to Mammy to make Abe a pair of buckskin breeches. Soon he would have a coonskin cap too, like Pappy's, and a pair of home-sewed moccasins to wear when the snow came.

It was two miles to the school where Caleb Hazel taught frontier children to read and write and cipher to the rule of three. Abe and his sister Sally joined the little group of boys and girls already seated on roughhewn benches in the log cabin, with only the dirt for a floor.

The cabin was dim. There were no windows, and the door must be left open to provide light. If there was little light, there was no lack of sound, for this was a "blab" school. Spelling, alphabet, arithmetic, all were learned by shouting aloud at the top of shrill voices, and schoolmaster Hazel had to have lungs of leather to make himself heard when he wished to speak.

Abe learned quickly. He and Sally had been to school for a few weeks the year before to Zachariah Riney, and already Abe could write his own name—Abraham Lincoln—and could spell out words from his teacher's battered blue-backed speller. His voice rose high in the babel of noise, everybody shouting, "Two times two is four. C-A-T spells cat."

After school Abe played in the road with his friend Austin Gollaher, until Sally caught him firmly by the hand and they started home. Sally was two years older and was put in charge of her little brother at school. She knew that Abe wanted to hunt walnuts and hickory nuts with Austin. Yesterday the boys had gone fishing at the hole in Knob Creek, where Abe had almost drowned once while swimming. He had caught one fish, but had given it to a weary soldier plodding home from fighting down south with General Andrew Jackson's army. Abe's father had told him to be good to soldiers, for they protected the country.

Abe and Sally went home to do the chores. Abe had to carry buckets of water for his mother, and bring in wood for the fireplace, and, when his father needed him, he helped on the farm. He was already old enough to ride the plow horse, and to drop seeds into freshly turned earth, or hoe out weeds when the corn sprouted.

Sometimes passing friends or strangers would stop for a short rest at the Lincoln cabin, which was on the main highway from Nashville to Louisville. Along the road past Tom Lincoln's clearing rattled white-topped wagons, filled with women, children, and household goods and driven by rough-voiced men who shouted at their slow teams of mules or oxen. Sometimes Abe

A replica of Abraham Lincoln's birthplace—a log cabin on Nolin Creek in Hardin (now La Rue) County, Kentucky.

watched one pull up, and heard a man call, "Howdy, folks, can you let us have a drink of water?"

Abe would fetch a gourd of water, and stand listening to talk of Indiana and of Illinois—new-broken wilderness to the north and west—and of the Indians. Abe heard plenty of talk, too, from the circuit-riding preacher, who sometimes hitched his horse to a tree in front of the cabin and stretched his tired legs out under the puncheon table as Nancy served him corn bread and fried hog meat. The preacher always read some passages from his worn Bible before he rode away.

Other times, when peddlers spread little stocks of needles and thread out, Nancy folded her rough red hands in her apron, and Abe and Sally knew that she was silently longing for these things. Tom Lincoln rode off to Hodgenville once in a while, and one exciting day returned with a few dishes and a wash-basin from an auction.

Down the road a piece lived some kinfolks, and when they came visiting Abe heard talk of the Lincolns, the Hankses, and the Sparrows. He held his breath in excitement whenever he heard his father tell how he had seen his own father, for whom Abe was named, killed by an Indian. Grandfather Abraham had brought his wife and three boys from Virginia along the Wilderness Road, following his friend Daniel Boone to Kentucky.

It was his mother's family, however, who lived nearby. Nancy Hanks Lincoln had been brought up by Betsy Sparrow, her aunt, and Betsy's husband, who were now raising Nancy's young cousin, Dennis Hanks. The Sparrows had also lived near Nancy and Tom when they had struggled to raise crops on a rocky farm eight miles from Knob Creek near the Sinking Spring. The Sinking Spring cabin was the birthplace of Abraham. It was nine-year-old Dennis who had held the baby in his arms on that cold February 12 in 1809, and it was Dennis who had handed him to Aunt Betsy Sparrow, saying, ''You take him, Aunt, he'll never come to much.''

Now, whenever Dennis saw Abe, he ruffled his cousin's coarse black hair and laughed, ''You're solemn as a papoose, Abe.''

This farm on the Cumberland Trail belonged to Tom Lincoln, for he had proved in court that he had the proper deed. Among the visitors Abe heard much talk of land deeds. There was the right kind and there was the wrong kind of deed—the pieces of paper that enabled rich men, who had large plantations and many slaves, to get possession of the farms of poor men. He heard his father tell how he had been brought before the law judge as a ''trespasser.'' What was a trespasser?

When Abe heard his father talk about the law, he wondered. Laws could be used against a poor man, who couldn't read and didn't know that he had the wrong kind of papers. Yet laws could protect Tom Lincoln, who had the right kind of deed. His father told him that the United States was built on laws. Laws were important. But that was a big word, that ''trespasser.''

Abe chewed solemnly on his supper of corn bread and fatback bacon, and thought about that long word. He had a thirst for learning. When he heard a word that he did not know or listened to talk that he did not understand, he was bothered. He had to know, he had to understand, and so he asked questions of everybody until he found out the meaning of the words.

His mother, Nancy, could not read or write. She knew verses from the Bible, and she sang the old hymns and the gay play-party songs. His father could not read either, but he could write his own name.

When Abe climbed into his chilly loft and lay down under a bearskin on his bed of corn shucks, he thought about words. The Knob Creek land was poor and barren, full of stones and washed by heavy rains that drained the topsoil away. Yet it was theirs, and they could live here because his father was not a trespasser and owned the land by law. As Abe's eyelids grew heavy with sleep he felt the wilderness night enfolding him. From far off in the canebrake came the scream of a panther, followed by the hoot of an owl, and, nearby, the restless movement of the heifer in her shed.

School days did not last long for Abe and Sally, for Tom Lincoln made up his mind to move to

Indiana. He had heard great tales of the rich soil and uncut timber north of the Ohio River. Indiana had just been admitted to the Union as a state where slavery was not permitted, and the government sold land there to settlers. Tom Lincoln thought that farming would be better in Indiana.

Abe helped his father build a flatboat. He held the planks as Tom sawed and shaped them, and when the boat was finished he shouted happily to see it splash into the water. Tom, who was a carpenter by trade, as well as a farmer, put his tools and some of the family furniture on board, along with several barrels of whisky for trading, since whisky was as good as money in the backwoods. Then Abe, with his mother and sister, watched silently as his father poled out of sight along Knob Creek toward the Ohio River.

Weeks later Tom returned on foot to say that he had found good land. The family immediately packed kettles, frying pan, and bedding, with some meal and bacon, on two horses, and set out. They traveled a hundred miles through the forests, across the Ohio River to their new land.

Tom had already cut the trees for a small clearing. There among the stumps the family hurried to build a pole shed, or "half-faced camp." As they chinked the three sides with mud, and put the roof on the shed, they shivered. The wind was sharp on their faces, and the last brown leaves of elm and oak drifted down on their heads. A fire made in the open side felt good to cold hands.

All that winter, as snow piled on the roof, the Lincolns lived in the camp. When spring came they started building a log cabin and planting newly cleared fields. The cabin had one room, a fireplace in a chimney made of stones and mud, and one door hung on leather hinges. There were no windows to light the dim shadows in corners, and sunlight came in only through the open door. Abe climbed every night into the loft, where he slept on a pile of corn shucks or dry leaves, wrapped in a bearskin, as he had done in Kentucky.

The hardest work was clearing fields. Day after day Tom Lincoln cut trees, hauled logs, and grubbed out and dragged away stumps. Trees seemed to cling to their soil with roots that would not let go. Abe learned that spring and summer to use an axe, bringing it down again and again until his arms ached. He knew the weariness that followed a day's hard labor with the endless tree stumps, and he slept afterwards as soundly as a bear in a cave.

One day in autumn, not long after the Lincolns had moved into their new cabin, they heard a long whoop echoing through the forest. It was the Sparrow family, come to join them in this wild country.

Tom and Betsy Sparrow with seventeen-year-old Dennis Hanks, moved into the old pole shed until they could clear land of their own. It was lonely out in the woods, sixteen miles from the nearest neighbor, and the Lincolns were happy to have their kinfolks with them. Happiness came unexpectedly to pioneer people sometimes, and sorrow came suddenly, too. That autumn the deadly illness called the "milksick" took both human beings and cattle. Tom and Betsy Sparrow died of it, and were buried in the woods near the deer run. Then Nancy, who had nursed them, became desperately ill. Soon there was another grave in the forest, where branches of beech and oak and walnut sighed in the wind.

The cabin in the clearing seemed an empty place to Abe and Sally. They were terribly alone in the room with the hard dirt floor and rough-cut furniture. Nobody talked much, and a deep sadness came to Abe's gray eyes.

Dennis Hanks moved in with them, and they all shared the work of cooking, hoeing, planting, and clearing. Sally was only twelve years old and it was easy to see that a woman was needed there.

Tom Lincoln got on his horse and journeyed back to Kentucky.

One day Abe's bare feet flew across the clearing. At his shout, Dennis came running from the woods, axe in hand, and Sally bounded through the cabin door. There was a creaking of wagon wheels, jingling of harness, and a loud shout from the trail. Abe stood speechless as he saw a wagon, four horses, and five people pull up in front of him. Tom jumped down and behind him came a strong, smiling woman.

"Here is your new mammy, Abe," said Tom Lincoln.

She was Sarah Bush Johnston, now Lincoln, a widow who had married Abe's father, and had brought along her three children, John, Sarah, and Matilda Johnston. She had brought, also, a big load of goods—walnut dresser, pillows, mattresses, tables and chairs, and a Bible. Abe shuffled his feet in the dust as he saw her eyes on his dirty clothes.

Before the sun set that evening the new mother had put everybody to work. The floor was cleaned, the kettles scrubbed, the clothes washed. One by one the children went into the horse trough with soft soap and water, and came out slicked and shining. The cabin had a woman's hand in it now and, with the new furniture and fixings, it looked like a palace to Abe and Sally.

From the first moment Abe liked his new mother, and she liked him. She was a warm-hearted, understanding woman. Frontier folk had a rough time keeping fed, warmed, clothed, and sheltered. They worked hard from sunup to sundown. Few had any interest in books and education, and reading was thought to be a sign of laziness and queerness. That was the way Tom Lincoln felt about it. Abe already knew how to read, write, and figure a little. Wasn't that enough? Sally Bush Lincoln didn't think so. She sent the children off to a school nine miles away. Teachers never stayed long in any of the schools, and when this one closed Abe went to another. His stepmother understood as no one else did how much he wanted to learn, even though schooling did not amount to much for teachers knew scarcely more than their pupils. Abe's entire school attendance never covered more than about a year of school days. He always said, ''I learned by littles.''

Yet Abe was learning many things. He spent days alone in the forest, felling trees, trimming branches, splitting rails. He had such long arms and legs that before he was seventeen he could handle an axe better than any man in the countryside. His strength grew, along with skill, until he could husk more corn than anybody, and in a wrestling match could throw any bully who tussled with him.

Folks said, "Abe Lincoln is as strong as three men," and they told how he had lifted a corncrib on his shoulders and carried it across a farmyard. They said that it took a big fellow to carry a four-hundred-pound corncrib. Abe was a big fellow. He grew to be six feet four inches tall, with muscles that let him hold an axe at arm's length straight and steady.

He believed in fair play, and when he thought a fight was getting out of hand he stepped in and flung the fighters apart. Abe could handle a situation, and that gave him confidence. Yet he had a certain deep humility, too. He had a mind, and he knew that this mind must grow strong with knowledge, just as his muscles grew strong with the great arching strokes of his axe.

Abe had a love for jokes. Once when his stepmother told him that if he didn't keep his hair clean he would ruin her ceiling, Abe walked a small boy in mud, and then held him upside down to make footprints across the white-washed ceiling. Sarah laughed, but made him give the ceiling a fresh coat of whitewash. Abe could laugh at himself as well as at others, and when a

Abe's father, Thomas Lincoln, was a hard-working farmer and carpenter who built a life for his family on the American frontier. Abe's stepmother, Sarah Bush Lincoln (seen here in 1865 at age 77), was warm and loving toward the boy.

laugh got hold of him it made him grab his knees with his arms and rock back and forth.

Life in the frontier country was hard, and there was nothing to stimulate ambition. Tom Lincoln was an average borderer, as pioneers were called, neither better nor worse than the general run of men who worked hard enough to get along, and no more than that. He had no thoughts beyond his daily living. Yet his son possessed a thirst for knowledge. He read all of the books that he could lay hands on, then he read them aloud both when alone and to others, and he asked questions about the things he read. He listened to others, and wanted to know what they thought.

Of a morning in summer he would stride across the fields with his axe in hand, and a book under his arm. His father often frowned as he watched him, for Abe distracted others with his book talk, and had to be called down for it. Yet Tom had a grudging pride in this gangling son who could write letters for the neighbors and explain things to them.

Among the trees Abe's axe made strong, steady sounds as it sank into the log. When the sun climbed to full noon the sounds stopped, and the tall boy dropped to the ground to eat his corn bread and bacon, and to read. He had read the books many times, but that didn't matter. Abe read slowly, and carefully, with the same quiet deliberation that he swung an axe. Nevertheless, he remembered what he read, and later in life he said of himself, ''My mind is like a piece of metal—hard to scratch anything on, and impossible to get it off after it is on.''

Squirrels frisked their fluffy tails about him, and a red fox perked up its ears in surprise at an unexpected sound. Abe was reading aloud. When the sun disappeared, leaving the sky beyond the trees stained with the purple and red of its passing, Abe went home. He stretched out in front of the hearth, and began to figure sums on a piece of board that was used to shovel ashes. He marked with a stick of burnt wood, and as he covered the board he studied his work. Then, satisfied, he shaved it off again with his knife, and started on another sum.

Dennis came in, sat down on a three-legged stool, and watched his cousin for a while. Then he said in a puzzled tone, "Abe, you are peculiar-some!"

Abe raised his eyes from under the overhanging mop of hair, and replied, "What I want to know is in books. My best friend is the man who'll get me a book I ain't read."

Yet when Dennis said that he was going to Gentry's store for a while after supper, his cousin thought that he would like to stretch his legs, too, and went along. Abe liked people as well as he liked books, and never missed a chance to join a crowd of men and boys. Gentryville, a mile and a half from the Lincoln cabin, was the little crossroads village where men sat of an evening listening to long Abe tell jokes that rocked them off their cracker barrels with laughter. "Abe can make a cat laugh," they said. Abe explained to them the books that he read, and he made knowledge plain to understand, and fun to listen to, by telling a story to illustrate every point. He said thoughtfully, "I want to bound my subject north, south, east, and west."

This young man who was given to laughter, and yet had a deep sadness in his nature—he was different from the other backwoods fellows. He made his decisions in the same way that he read a book, slowly, thoughtfully. And, having made them, he did not forget. He said of himself, "I am a slow walker, but I never turn back."

One night during a storm, driving rain came through a chink in the log cabin, up in the loft, and almost ruined the book that he had borrowed from Josiah Crawford. It was Parson Weems's *Life of Washington*. When Abe saw it next day, he tucked the wet book under his arm and swung his legs down the road to the Crawfords'. Abe worked hard pulling fodder for Crawford for two days to pay for the damage, and when he finished Josiah Crawford surprised him by giving the book to him for his own.

Young Lincoln walked to cabins for miles around to borrow books. He read everything that he could get his hands on: the Bible, Aesop's Fables, *Pilgrim's Progress,* and any school-book that he could find. But his favorite was the *Life of Washington*. He read the rain-soaked book until he knew it by heart.

If books were hard to come by in the frontier country, paper was even more so. Dennis knew that Abe wanted a notebook in which he could jot down his thoughts, write a rough poem once in a while, and copy poems that he especially liked. And so when Dennis had a chance to get some sheets of clean white paper, he brought them home to his cousin, who sewed them together to make his first notebook. Into the crude book went poems, thoughts on many subjects, and an essay on national politics saying, "The American government is the best form of government in the world for an intelligent people. It ought to be kept sacred and preserved forever."

He wrote also that "education should be fostered, the Constitution must be held sacred,—the Union must be perpetuated,—and the laws must be revered, respected and enforced." These were the things that he kept thinking about.

On Sundays the Lincolns went a mile down the road to Pigeon Creek church, a log building built by the settlers themselves among the trees. To reach it people walked or rode for many miles and sat all day on rough benches, listening to the preaching, reading Bible verses, and singing the well-known hymns that their fathers and mothers had sung before them. At dinnertime under the trees they talked of local affairs and politics.

Sometimes Abe went to church meetings, and sometimes he stayed at home with his books. The day after a church service Abe could mount a stump and while the other children listened, preach as good a sermon as the parson.

When Abe was not working for his father, he worked for farmers around Gentryville, doing whatever job was needed—plowing, splitting rails, or killing hogs. The first time he asked for a job killing hogs the farmer answered, "Think you can do it, Abe?"

"Well," laughed Abe, "I'll risk myself if you'll risk the hog." Abe always brought his pay to his father, for a frontier boy was not his own master until he was twenty-one.

When he was about seventeen he rowed a homemade ferry boat on the Ohio River, taking passengers out to river boats. One day two travelers hailed him. Abe loaded the men, with their trunks, into the boat and rowed them to the steamer. When they were on board the men threw him two half dollars. Abe was so astonished at this wealth, more than he had ever made at one time before, that he let one silver piece slip from his fingers. As he saw it sink out of sight in the brown water he had a feeling of despair, for he had not known that it was possible to make so much so easily, and lose it so quickly.

Running the ferry gave Abe another experience when two boatmen with a rival ferry hailed Abe into court in Kentucky on the other side of the river. They said that Abe had broken the law, which required a Kentucky license for a ferry operating across the river. Abe convinced Judge Pate that he had not ''for reward set any person over a river,'' but had only taken his passengers to steamers in midstream. The judge dismissed the charge, and he and Abe Lincoln became friends. After that Abe went to court sometimes, and watched and listened. Law was important. It could befriend a poor man—if understood.

When Abraham Lincoln was nineteen years old he was offered a chance to see the outside world beyond his wilderness. For two years he had watched river steamers, flatboats, and rafts swinging down the current on the Ohio River. He had talked from time to time with rivermen, rough and wild, with traveling preachers, with pioneer families, always moving westward, and with gamblers, hunters, and peddlers. He saw them only briefly as they went by. Then James Gentry, the most prosperous farmer of the Pigeon Creek region, hired Abe to make a flatboat, take a cargo to New Orleans, and sell it there. Abe's assistant was to be Gentry's son, Allen.

Toward spring Abe went to work cutting oak

planks, and when breezes blew warmer across the river, and water was running high, he finished his flatboat. It had a deck shelter, two sets of oars, and a steering pole. The boys loaded the boat with its cargo of corn, potatoes, and hams, and pushed off downriver.

Young Lincoln was venturing out into the world for the first time. His only knowledge of the East had been gained from books and from the people passing on the river. From the East there was a constant flow of humanity down the rivers that were the great highways of the time. From the British Isles and from all of the countries of Europe, as well as from the seaboard states, people traveled the Ohio River. It carried commerce and trade, and it governed the lives of all those who lived within miles of it.

As the flatboat floated down the stream the boys watched for a sight of notorious Cave-in-Rock, where river pirates lured boatmen into stopping for a drink of rum, and then, so the story goes, murdered them for their goods. The Ohio carried the flatboat to the Mississippi, and on down to New Orleans—a thousand miles from home. Sometimes the boys poled alongside snags and sandbars, or were carried slowly by the current on the muddy waters of the wide river. At night they tied up at the shore and slept uneasily, with hand on gun or club. Travel was dangerous, for the coves and inlets harbored thieves and pirates. Past the flatboat churned gilded steamboats, glittering with lights—proud queens of the mighty Mississippi.

One night near the end of their run, as Abe and Allen slept on the flatboat, which was tied up at the shore near a Louisiana sugar plantation, a gang of seven homeless blacks crept on board to kill them and steal the cargo. Abe and Allen fought the thieves with clubs and drove them off in a battle during which Abe knocked several into the water. He received a cut over the eye that gave him a scar for life. The boys hastily pushed off into the stream, and put as much distance between the bandits and themselves as possible. In New Orleans they disposed of their potatoes, hams, and corn, and then sold the flatboat for lumber.

After a few days in New Orleans they returned by steamboat to Indiana. Abe knew that he was a comical sight in his home-spun shirt, coonskin cap, and buckskin breeches that had shrunk in the rains until the legs cut into his shins, making blue marks. But it did not matter, for he was used to seeing people laugh at his ungainly appearance. He was also used to the astonished looks he got when he began to talk.

His head was packed with the sights and sounds and varied smells of river life and of New Orleans. Back in Gentryville he looked and laughed and talked as usual, except that now he had more stories to tell. He could talk of the river pirates, or the sailors in the streets of New Orleans, or the mixture of foreign languages and the varied kinds of clothes there. He could also tell of the slave markets, where he had seen men, women, and children sold at auction to the highest bidders, like so many cattle.

Often pioneers were unsettled, restless people. They felt that always just beyond the westward horizon there must be a land where living was easier. Tom Lincoln had not found Indiana as productive as he had hoped, and the "milksick" was raging again. The Lincoln and Hanks clan received word of richer land in Illinois. A few years earlier a cousin, John Hanks, who had followed them to Indiana from Kentucky, had gone on into Illinois, and when spring came in 1830 his kinfolks decided to move there also.

Abe helped his father make a wagon. Dennis and Levi Hall, who had married Abe's stepsisters, were going also, and as talk continued about Illinois, more of the family joined in the plans. Abe's own sister, Sally, was not one of them, for she had married when Abe was eighteen, and had been buried a year later with her newborn child. Abraham was twenty-one years old now, and no longer under his father's orders. He accompanied the seventeen members of his family to Illinois, and helped drive the seven-yoke team of young steers. Abe also bought a little stock of pins, needles, and thread, and peddled them along the way to put some cash money into his jeans.

The Lincolns settled near John Hanks, but soon moved farther away to Goose Nest Prairie, where they found their lasting homes. All but Abe—who was footloose, restless, and anxious to be on his own. At the home of John Hanks he met a man named Denton Offut, who took an instant liking to Abe. Offut was an energetic man, talkative, and filled with grand notions and plans for making money. He was not a man to think carefully or work hard at anything. He asked Abe, John Hanks, and John Johnston to take a flatboat loaded with barrels of pork to New Orleans.

The three men built the flatboat, loaded it, and floated down the narrow Sangamon River. When the boat rounded the curve at New Salem Village, it stuck on the Rutledge milldam, and hung there, slowly filling with water. Villagers sat on the bank and shouted advice as they watched the tall young fellow who moved slowly and awkwardly.

"What's he going to do now?"

"He'll never save her!"

Abe called to one of the men, and asked for the loan of a rowboat for a little while. When the boat pulled alongside him Abe unloaded his cargo into it. Still the flatboat hung there, with water inside. What would that long, lanky fellow do now? They watched as he bored a hole in the boat, in the end that hung over the dam, and drained the water out. Then he plugged the hole securely, dropped the flatboat down over the dam and reloaded her again.

Once more Abe was leaving his land of trees and farms and clay roads for the traffic of the river. In New Orleans he stared again at the network of narrow streets, and at the people who looked so strange to him. Once more he stood on the wharves looking up at countless masts of ships from all the world outlined against the sky. In the city he watched trading in food, furs, cotton, and timber, as well as trafficking in dark-skinned human lives.

When Abe had worked his way back upstream by firing the furnace on a river steamer, he said good-by for good to his home with his father and stepmother. He had never had any companionship with his father, but his affection for Sarah Bush Lincoln was to be lifelong. Abraham paddled down the Sangamon in a homemade canoe, to take a job in New Salem in a store that Denton Offut was ready to open.

New Salem was a village of log cabins, on a bluff where the river made a curve. It was about the same size when Abe came there in 1831 as another village called Chicago, located on Lake Michigan. Abe arrived on election day and wandered over to the cabin where the voting was going on.

"Say, you stranger, can you write? We need help with this voting."

Lincoln's wide mouth spread in a grin that made his eyes twinkle, as he drawled, "I reckon I can make a few rabbit tracks," and sat down to write the names of the voters as they spoke their preferences. As he made his "rabbit tracks" this odd-looking newcomer told stories and soon had a guffawing crowd of men listening.

When Offut arrived in New Salem he and Abe built a log cabin for a store and stocked the shelves with goods for sale. Abe Lincoln liked people and they liked him. He lived first with one friend and then with another. He liked his friends for their different qualities. There was Mentor Graham, the school-teacher, who helped Abe study grammar, mathematics, and Shakespeare. Reverend Cameron liked Lincoln, and James

Rutledge, who owned the mill and ran a tavern in a four-room house, was a companion. Bowling Green was soon a good friend, but Abe Lincoln had to fight his way to friendship with the Clary's Grove boys.

The young men who lived at Clary's Grove were tough. They boasted that they could win any fight ever started, and their champion was Jack Armstrong. This Abe Lincoln looked strong too, but he was queer in some ways. He wouldn't drink or play cards, and he didn't like to hunt. Denton Offut bragged about Abe and told everybody he met that Lincoln could out-wrestle, out-fight a Clary's Grove boy anytime.

"Let's see him throw Jack then!"

Abe was willing to oblige. Jack and Abe faced each other outside of the Offut store as a crowd pushed in around them. Jack advanced like a cock of the roost and made a grab for Abe. The crowd began to howl and yell, "Get a hold on him, Jack. Tussle him!"

Jack couldn't seem to do it. This fellow had arms that were so long and strong that nobody could get close to him. Then Jack stamped on Abe's foot, and Abe grabbed the Clary's Grove champion, shook him as a dog shakes a bone, and slammed him down flat on his back in the dirt.

The whole gang from Clary's Grove advanced on the newcomer, who stood with feet planted solidly on the earth, unmoving. Jack Armstrong pulled himself to his feet, wiped his face, and shouted at them to let Lincoln alone.

"He's won in a fair fight, and he's the best fellow that ever came here."

From then on Abe and Jack Armstrong were friends, and Abe often stayed with Jack and his motherly wife, Hannah, at Clary's Grove.

Abe was still "peculiarsome." Although he wrestled with the boys, judged their cockfights, ran races and won, and threw the maul farther than anybody—still, much of his time was spent reading any book he could get hold of. He walked for miles to borrow books, and brought them home tied in his red bandanna on the end of a stick. There was so much that he didn't know. Fortunately storekeeping gave him a good deal of time for reading.

He could often stretch out on the long counter for hours with a book before his eyes, and he could count on not being interrupted too often by a demand for a pound of sugar, or a jug of whisky, because the Offut store was not doing well. The store cat jumped up beside him, to curl into a furry ball in the curve of his arm. The sound of purring rose and fell and was joined by a buzzing of bees around the syrup jug on the floor. When he finished a book his first thought was, "Where can I get another one?"

What should he study next? He had ideas about what would improve this Sangamon country—better education, navigation of the river, and maybe a railroad? He thought about laws, and now he was thinking of lawmaking. Why shouldn't he run for the state legislature? Some of his friends told him that he should.

A customer came in and Abe untangled his legs, swinging them down from the counter. He reached for scissors and a bolt of turkey-red calico. As he spoke his slow "Howdy" and asked about the children, his mind was still busy with a thought. Why not run for office? It was pretty certain that this store would "wink out" soon anyway.

Everybody talked about river trade, and Abe heard that the little steamer, the *Talisman*, was to be put on a regular run from St. Louis on the Mississippi to Springfield on the Sangamon. He asked for a job as assistant to the pilot, and was hired when the Offut store really had "winked out."

The trip up the Sangamon in the spring when water ran high was a success, and it brought cheers from the villagers as well as from townspeople at Springfield. But the return trip down was a different matter. The water level had dropped to such an extent by that time that the *Talisman* was in trouble. In New Salem people watched unhappily as part of the Rutledge dam had to be removed to get the steamer over. Navigation on this narrow river was a failure, and Lincoln was out of a job again.

As he was casting about for something to do he heard much talk about Black Hawk, the famous old Indian chief. Indians had gone westward out of Illinois some years before, but now Black Hawk and a band of braves had crossed back into Illinois, with the explanation that they needed land to raise corn there. Settlers along the Mississippi reported that Black Hawk had five hundred braves with him, and that they were a menace to the borderers, who were angry. A shooting war started and United States regulars were sent into the region to protect lonely settlers in their cabins. A call was sent out for local volunteers also. Abe Lincoln, along with most of the Clary's Grove boys and other young men from New Salem, enlisted.

Volunteers elected their own officers by vote. When Lincoln and another man from the village stood out, the men lined up behind them, thus indicating their preference. The tall clerk from

Offut's store won out. Lincoln said later that few things in his life had pleased him as much as that election. He was completely ignorant of military knowledge, but he was a captain who had the respect of his men. At first he went on foot as all of his officially designated "mounted brigade" did—for lack of horses—but later he rode on a mount that he bought with his first pay.

One day when Captain Lincoln was drilling his backwoodsmen, he marched them through a field, twenty abreast. When they approached a fence with a narrow gate, the captain was stumped for a few minutes. He didn't know the correct command.

"Halt!" he shouted. "The company will break ranks for two minutes and form again on the other side of the gate."

The New Salem volunteers did a great deal of marching, but never saw a live and hostile Indian. However, not far from a place called Kellog's Grove, Lincoln's men found the bodies of five soldiers who had been killed and scalped there the day before.

One night as his men sat around their campfire, growling about their empty stomachs, Lincoln looked up to see an old Indian standing quietly nearby. At that moment two other men saw the stranger and reached for their guns.

"Indians! It's the redskins!"

The Indian did not move as soldiers rushed forward toward him. He was the first Indian that they had seen since enlisting.

"Kill him!" somebody shouted.

The captain moved forward and stood in front of the old Indian, who was holding in his hand a safe-conduct pass from General Cass.

"No, you won't kill him," said Lincoln.

"You're a coward, Lincoln," shouted one of the men.

"If any man thinks I am a coward, let him prove it. You can choose the weapons."

The men moved back and muttered angrily, but they let the old Indian go peacefully away.

At the end of thirty days many of the men went home, but Lincoln re-enlisted. "I am out of work," he said with a laugh, "and there being no danger of more fighting, I can do nothing better than enlist again." By July Black Hawk had been ambushed and captured by the United States regulars, and the Indian war was over. Lincoln returned to New Salem hungry and on foot, for his horse had been stolen.

Although he was poor and unemployed he was a candidate for the legislature, having announced his candidacy just before he had volunteered by sending out a circular to the voters. He

was running as a Whig against old Peter Cartwright, the tough and hot-tongued Methodist
preacher. Abe started campaigning at once. He
helped farmers harvest their crops and he talked
with them about their problems. They thought
that he talked sense, both in the fields and in his
speeches.

To wind up the campaign Lincoln went to Papp-
ville to make a speech. It was auction day and a
crowd was milling about the square, where
farmers herded squealing pigs and bawling cattle,
enveloped in clouds of dust. Lincoln found a box
strong enough to hold him, and stepped up on it.
With his head well above the crowd, he could see
everything that was going on.

As he raised his voice over the din he saw a
fight starting between a rowdy and a man who
was one of his friends. He stepped down from his
box, pushed through the throng, grabbed the
rowdy by the neck and the seat of his pants, and
tossed him ten feet. Then he returned to his
"platform." There was a sudden silence.

"Fellow citizens," he began, "I presume you
all know who I am. I am humble Abraham Lincoln. I have been solicited by many friends to
become a candidate for the legislature. My politics are short and sweet, like the old woman's
dance. I am in favor of a national bank. I am in

favor of the internal improvements system and a high protective tariff. These are my sentiments and political principles. If elected I shall be thankful; if not, it will be all the same.''

When election day came he was glad to know that his own New Salem precinct had voted for him, although he had not been elected. And so, back in New Salem he wondered once again what to do with himself. Should he become a blacksmith? He had the muscular arms for it. What he wanted to do most was to be a lawyer, but how could he? He had no education, except the kind that he picked up ''by littles,'' as he said—like a squirrel gathering a store of nuts for the winter.

For a while he did odd jobs for his friends, and his friends were many, of all ages. When he saw a small boy chopping wood in freezing weather, and heard that he was doing this to earn enough to buy shoes for his bare feet, Abe sent him in to the warmth of a stove and chopped the wood for him. When he saw a pig struggling hopelessly in a swamp and was tempted to pass by because he was wearing his best jeans, he waded in anyway and pulled the animal from the mud. When his friends needed help Abe cut wood, plowed a field, or minded a baby. He went to turkey shoots and took part in contests of strength and skill, and at square dances in the schoolhouse watched the young men and girls "Skip to My Lou" to the bouncing music of fiddles.

William Berry was a friend who asked Lincoln to go in with him on his general store when his partner offered to sell out. Together they bought up old stock from another store that was going out of business and set up as Berry and Lincoln. Berry spent most of his time in the tavern, while Lincoln waited on his few customers in the little store. Surrounded by the mingled smells of rawhide boots, chicken feed, molasses and apples, Abe again collected all the books that he could borrow and read them.

Lincoln was too obliging to be a good storekeeper, since he refused to force payment of a bill and would not turn down anybody who was in real need. As the weeks passed his mind grew rich with knowledge of Shakespeare and Burns, gleaned from his dreamy-eyed friend, Jack Kelso. Jack liked fishing, so Abe, who was neither a hunter nor a fisherman, sat with him on the riverbank and took turns with him reading aloud from Jack's old copies of Burns's poems and Shakespeare's plays. As Lincoln's mind became richer with knowledge, his purse grew leaner.

One day a covered wagon rattled into the village and came to a creaking halt before the store. Lincoln called, "Howdy, stranger."

The bearded man who was driving asked Lincoln to buy an old barrel of junk that he had with him. To help the man Lincoln handed him a half dollar, although he had no use for the barrel. As the wagon rolled away he shrugged at himself, then he leaned over and noticed that there seemed to be a book in the bottom. He took it out and saw with amazement and delight that he had in his hand a copy of Blackstone. This was a book that every lawyer must learn. It held the foundation laws of the English-speaking-world. He held it before him and stared at it. Never had he thought he would own it. Right away he went to his favorite reading spot, the counter, stretched out on it, and plunged into the study of law.

Less and less did Lincoln join the boys in wrestling matches, at races and trials of physical skill. His nose was buried in Blackstone. He went often to talk with Dr. Allen, a religious man who had strong convictions on the evils of slavery and the evils of drink. Abe was not only reading and studying, but thinking too.

The store went more and more into debt. Berry seldom came around to work in it and Abe, who had also the job of postmaster, was often away from it. When he knew that some farm wife wanted a letter from her faraway son he took it to her even if it meant a walk of five miles. Lincoln formed a habit of carrying letters and any paper of value in his old felt hat—the one that had been black but was now, as he said, "just a combine of colors."

After a while debt became so pressing that Lincoln knew he had to get outside work. He took temporary jobs at the mill, or splitting rails, or harvesting corn. Yet these jobs did not pay enough to help him meet his debts. Then he heard that a man named Calhoun in Springfield, the chief surveyor in that area, was much in need of an assistant to help him clear land titles for settlers on the prairies.

Lincoln knew no more about surveying than the store cat, yet he thought that if he could learn law and Kirkham's grammar and mathematics— then he could also learn surveying. He walked to Springfield, saw Calhoun, borrowed a book on surveying from him, and said that he would be able to go to work in six weeks. Mrs. Calhoun stood on the porch and watched that tall, ungainly figure walk away with the surveying book tied in a red bandanna on a stick held over his shoulder.

"That's the queerest-looking man I ever saw."

Her husband looked after Lincoln and said slowly, "For all that, he is no common man."

Lincoln went back to the village, to spend

every minute of the day, and much of the night, learning this difficult subject. It was extremely hard work for him. Mentor Graham, the school-master, helped him, but Abe's eyes seemed to sink deeper into their sockets with fatigue and he looked ill. He had to learn the use of chain and compass and tripod—mathematical formulas, angles, and measuring. Nobody thought he could do it.

Nevertheless, in six weeks he knew how to survey the land. He got a horse, borrowed money to buy a set of instruments, and rode off into the woods to work. His first pay was two buckskins, which Hannah Armstrong, Jack's wife at Clary's Grove, ''foxed'' onto his pants legs, to protect them from briars.

Sometimes he made three dollars a day, in real money, but he did not have work regularly. Debts grew higher. Berry died and Lincoln was responsible for payment. He was sued, and lost his horse and surveying instruments, which were sold at auction.

A farmer, James Short, bought them and gave them back to Lincoln. Abe gave the horse a pat, saying nothing for a few minutes, and then he turned to his friend with a warm smile.

''Uncle Jimmy, I'll do as much for you some-time.''

Without a store of his own, and with debts amounting to more than a thousand dollars, Lincoln went to work for Sam Hill, as store clerk and postmaster. He took his meals at the Rutledge Tavern, and was served there by Mrs. Rutledge and her girls. One of them was Ann, of the red-gold hair and the sweet voice. James Rutledge and John Cameron had built the mill and the first houses of New Salem Village. For a time these two were the most prosperous men there. Lincoln liked Rutledge, who was a Whig, and shared his political views.

Although Lincoln was an easy leader of men and the center of every male group, with women he was shy, and conscious of his lack of social graces, and of his poor clothing. He had known well only the wives of his friends—Hannah Armstrong, Nancy, wife of Bowling Green, the round little justice of the peace, and Jack Kelso's wife. Now he looked at Ann Rutledge with new eyes.

Lincoln knew that Ann was promised to John McNeil, a man from New York State who was rapidly buying up farms and becoming the rich man of the village. Suddenly McNeil left for his former home, leaving behind him whispers and suspicious rumors about his actions in the village.

When Ann came to the Hill store, Lincoln's

rugged face softened as he said, "Howdy, Miss Ann. What can I do for you today?"

But he dreaded the moment when, after she had bought a spool of white thread and a pound of sugar, she would finger her sunbonnet and ask, "Is there a letter for me, Mr. Lincoln?"

The situation was strange, for Lincoln had helped McNeil with a deed for property, and knew that his real name was McNamar. While in New Salem, McNeil had bought the Rutledge farm at Sand Ridge. Ann gradually stopped asking for the letter that did not come, and wrote to McNeil that she considered the engagement broken. She received no answer.

While Lincoln was working for Sam Hill he ran for the Illinois legislature again, and this time he won. Turning his pockets inside out, he found mighty little money in them. Abe looked down his long frame at his clothes. How could he go to the state legislature in patched, faded homespun trousers, held up by one suspender, in an old shirt, and a hat that was a "combine of colors"? He went out to see a farmer named Coleman Smoot.

"Did you vote for me, Smoot?" asked Lincoln.

"Yes, I did, Abe."

"Then will you lend me two hundred dollars? I want to buy some clothes and fix up a little."

Dressed in a new outfit—hat, bluejeans and shirt—Lincoln went to the village of Vandalia, capital of Illinois, where he started his political life. He boarded at Charter's Tavern, with some of the other legislators. Lincoln went there as one of four representatives from Sangamon County. In the legislative sessions he said little during the first term, but he listened and learned.

Abraham Lincoln had lived all of his life with backwoods farmers and villagers. Now, for the first time, he was getting acquainted with townspeople—people who had knowledge that went out and beyond the borders of their home fields. They talked of national politics, of music, of books, of railroad building, and of the things that were happening in the world. Although talk of the world at large came into Vandalia, the legislature itself was more concerned with local affairs and especially with transportation. This new state, still on the fringe of the wild West, was anxious for better means of getting crops to markets, and of bringing in goods from the East. Canals, rivers, and railroads were important subjects, and every growing town wanted the legislature to aid in getting transportation to it. Lincoln voted for a measure authorizing the building of the Illinois and Michigan Canal, and also for a bill to charter a state bank.

The session lasted two and a half months, and when it ended Lincoln rode home to New Salem in bitter February weather, convinced more than ever that he must become a lawyer. The law was the right approach to politics. He wanted to get into politics, and now believed that he might do so. He borrowed law books in Vandalia and in Springfield and studied them.

He came home to Ann Rutledge too. As winter gave way to spring, and the prairies turned green and wild flowers bloomed golden in the fields about New Salem, Abraham Lincoln and Ann Rutledge fell in love. Prospects for marriage were decidedly not good. Ann's father was now so poor that he had to sell his tavern and move his family to the log cabin on the farm that no longer belonged to them, to remain until they heard from McNeil, the absent owner. Lincoln rode out to see Ann, who was working that summer for Uncle Jimmy Short on a farm nearby.

The hot months brought trouble to New Salem Village, and to the farms all around. Out of the heat and the swamps came malaria, and then typhoid. Ann and her father were taken ill. Lincoln came and sat beside Ann as she grew weaker. Two days later she died. Her father lived only a short time after.

Lincoln's long face, where sadness seemed to

make its home, grew lined and etched with grief. In his twenty-six years he had lost his mother, his sister, and now the girl Ann. These two had made great plans for the autumn. She was to have gone to a school for girls and he to a college while he served his term in the legislature.

Lincoln's friends worried about him. He was lost in grief, wandering about unable to think, unable to work. Nancy and Bowling Green took him into their home, and put an axe in his big hands. Out under the sky, sinking his axe blade in a log, stripping the ripened ears of corn, and driving a team, he found help, while their friendship gave him comfort.

For a time Lincoln was ill in his turn, burning with fever and shaking with the chills of malaria. And then he was well again, weak, thin, tired, but willing to take up his life where he had left it. He went back, in the late fall, to the legislature at Vandalia. When the session was over in January, Lincoln was riding out again on horseback, and, with his surveying instruments, was striding through the tall prairie grasses laying out the boundaries of the land.

Lincoln was re-elected to the state legislature for the next term and went back to Vandalia as one of seven representatives who, with two senators from Sangamon County, were called the "Long Nine" because their combined height came to about fifty-four feet. This group was the largest from a county and the delegation went to Vandalia determined to move the state capital to Springfield. The session lasted three months, and when the "Long Nine" returned to Sangamon County they brought success. Springfield was to be the new capital.

Springfield was the growing town of southern Illinois. By 1836 New Salem was beginning to show signs of the gradual abandonment that was to obliterate it as a village, and return the land to the prairie and the forest.

The village called Chicago, on Lake Michigan, was growing like a husky western youth, unable to find clothing big enough to fit. But the Sangamon was not to be a river of commerce and Springfield, in a more central location than New Salem, was the coming town of that area.

In April of the year 1837, Abraham Lincoln left his good friends in New Salem and rode slowly to Springfield on a horse borrowed from Bowling Green. He had been a part of the village during most of its lifetime, for he came soon after it was built, and now it looked as if the village would not long outlast his leaving. The tall youth with the sad eyes and humorous mouth, who had wrestled, played marbles with children, clerked, and read books here, was now a man on his way to a law practice. He had mastered, on his own, the difficult profession of lawyer.

He was twenty-eight years old, and in this village he left his youth—the bite of an axe in a log, the friendship of an easygoing farm people, the grave of a girl with golden-red hair and a quiet smile.

Lincoln rode into Springfield with no possessions except the few personal belongings in his saddlebags, a little money in his pocket, a load of debt on his mind, and an arranged partnership with a lawyer, John T. Stuart, whom he had first met during the Black Hawk war.

Stuart had liked Lincoln ever since their campaigning days in the Indian war, and had loaned him law books to study while Lincoln lived in New Salem before his election. When Stuart's partner left his law firm Lincoln was asked to take his place. Stuart was also a politician, and the leader of the Whig party in Springfield.

Lincoln walked into the store of Joshua Speed, laid his saddlebags on the counter, and asked, "Now, what would you say the trappings for a single bedstead would cost?"

Speed stared at the stranger, and replied thoughtfully, "I reckon maybe about seventeen dollars would do it."

This young man's face, thought the store-keeper, was the saddest that he had ever seen, and he felt sorry for the man, without knowing why.

Lincoln spoke slowly. "It is probably cheap enough; but I want to say that, cheap as it is, I have not the money to pay. But if you will credit me until Christmas, and if my experiment here as a lawyer is a success, I will pay you then. If I fail in that I will probably never pay you at all."

Speed took an instant liking to this stranger, with his honesty and his frankness. He told Lincoln that he would be glad to have him share his double bed over the store, and then he need not go into debt at all. They looked at each other, and smiled. From that moment, they were lifelong friends.

Lincoln's partner's practice was large, though not rich in fees, and Lincoln was busy every day at the courthouse or in the office. In the evenings he sat in Speed's store with a group of men, talking politics. He had little contact with social life, but did not mind this, as he never had felt at home in a drawing room, and had few of the social graces that ladies admired.

When Stuart decided to run for the Congress of the United States, Lincoln assumed most of the duties of the firm. He also made election speeches for his law partner. People began to talk about Lincoln, about his straight thinking and his good stories.

His friends told how a Democrat named Taylor spoke hotly of the aristocracy of the Whigs, and how Lincoln, with a sudden quirk to the side of his wide mouth, rose and ripped open the speaker's tightly buttoned shirt. Out fell a lot of lacy ruffles—a sure sign of aristocracy. The crowd howled with glee, and from that day the man was known as "Ruffled Shirt Taylor," and his charge of Whig aristocracy was lost in the laughter.

Southern Illinois was just across the Ohio River from Kentucky—a slave state and a free state separated by a stream of brown water. Lincoln knew that beliefs and ideas and feelings were not separated by a river. There were people in northern Kentucky who did not believe in slavery and some in southern Illinois who agreed with the southern point of view. The more thoughtful people of Springfield were close enough to the South to feel the conflict coming.

Ninian Edwards, of the Long Nine, was one of the prominent citizens of Springfield who had southern connections. His wife was a Kentuckian, and the social leader of the town. When the legislature met there for the first time the Edwardses gave a grand ball, and the guest of honor was Miss Mary Todd, sister of the hostess.

Lincoln went to the ball, and could not take his eyes off the plump, pretty girl with dark hair and blue eyes. She waltzed gracefully, spoke French, had the social manners that he lacked, and a sparkling, pointed wit that kept everyone circling around her.

Lincoln approached her and said, ''Miss Todd, I want to dance with you the worst way.''

Mary told her sister later, with a laugh, that he certainly did, too. But, for all of his awkward ways, she liked him very much. He had a quality that made her believe in him. There was that about him, somehow, which spoke of a future. After some months of friendship and then courtship, Mary Todd and Abraham Lincoln were betrothed.

Then Lincoln's doubts began to come. He was poor, he was awkward socially. Should he marry? This fine young Southern belle was attractive, but she did have a violent temper, and a very sharp tongue. Did he actually want to marry?

When the date for the wedding approached, Lincoln's thoughts were so uncertain that he fell again into one of the fits of melancholy that were

Lincoln was married to Mary Todd, a Kentucky belle, on November 4, 1842. This photo was taken at his presidential inauguration in 1861—by which time she had borne four sons.

like dark seas sweeping over his spirit. He told Mary of his doubts, and they quarreled. The engagement was broken. Mary hid her feelings, and went out to parties with other escorts.

Lincoln's depression grew worse, until, as he said to Stuart, "I am now the most miserable man living." His friends advised him to go away for a while. Instead, he continued to work. Joshua Speed moved to Kentucky and married. He wrote Lincoln that he was happy in his new home and new work. Lincoln felt that if Speed could marry happily so could he.

A meeting between Mary Todd and Lincoln was arranged by a friend without their previous knowledge. Abraham Lincoln and Mary Todd were married quietly at the home of Ninian Edwards, in Springfield, on November 4, 1842. They went to live in the Globe Hotel for some months, until they could buy a home. A few days after the marriage Lincoln ended a letter to a friend by writing, "Nothing new here, except my marriage, which, to me, is a matter of profound wonder."

Mr. and Mrs. Lincoln lived in the hotel until the birth of their first son, Robert, late in summer. Then they moved into a house that they bought from the Reverend Dresser, who had performed their marriage ceremony.

After a few years Lincoln left Stuart's law firm

and joined Judge Logan, who was one of the best lawyers in Illinois. Judge Logan was thought to be the most careless man in Springfield in his dress, but he was careful in his law practice. He taught Lincoln to spend time on preparation of his cases, to keep his papers in order, and to know his facts. Lincoln learned much from him.

Traveling from town to town and court to court, as a country lawyer had to do, was also valuable to him. He had all sorts of cases; he defended boys who got in trouble in fights, helped men collect damages, assisted women to hold their property. He made out deeds, and was occasionally prosecutor in a criminal case. He helped freed slaves defend their rights in a free state and also assisted a slave owner to recover a runaway slave.

The time came, however, when Lincoln felt that he should be more on his own. When Judge Logan's son was ready to join his father Lincoln agreed to step out. He then asked a younger man, William Herndon, to be his partner. Herndon always called his partner Mr. Lincoln, and Lincoln called him Billy.

"Billy," he said, "I can trust you if you can trust me."

They were very different men. Herndon was quick to anger and had abolitionist views. Lincoln was calm and deliberate and a moderate in his thinking. He was still, as he said, "a slow walker who never turned back." They became close friends, sharing a dusty office on the second floor of Hoffman's Row, on the town square.

Lincoln spent much of his time riding his gray horse from town to town on the Eighth Judicial Circuit. His saddlebags carried extra clothing, and a few books and papers. He often read a book as his horse jogged along the roads that were dusty or muddy, according to the weather.

Now he was no longer called Abe, but was Mr. Lincoln to everybody. He dressed differently, too, in black broadcloth suits, white shirts, and black silk cravats. The old felt hat of many weathered hues had been replaced by a high silk "stove-pipe" hat. But Mr. Lincoln still held his trousers up with one suspender, or "gallus," as he called it, and he still carried important papers in his hat. His hair refused to stay down, and his trouser legs had a way of rising above his bony ankles. He still looked, as his father had once said, as if he needed a carpenter's plane to smooth him down.

Lawyer Lincoln was often so slow to decide a question in his mind that people thought him lazy. He sat sometimes in his office, looking out of the window toward the prairies as quietly as a tree stands in the forest when the air is motionless. Around Mr. Lincoln the office was dusty, so dusty that at one time seeds left in a corner began to sprout tiny pale green spears pointing toward the light slanting in through the window.

Herndon talked of abolishing slavery, cutting it out of the nation completely. He spoke angrily of laws that permitted men to enslave other men. This was an issue that was all-important to the United States of America, since it concerned not only the slaves but also questions of moral right and wrong, of Constitutional and legal rights, of a way of life, and of the future of the nation.

Lincoln knew that this question was not an easy one. Washington and Jefferson had not believed in slavery. In 1808 the bringing of slaves to American shores had been forbidden by law, but slave ships were still bringing cargoes from Africa and blacks were being smuggled into the South, to be sold at auction. In the North blacks were usually house servants and were free by law.

The invention of machines, the building up of factories, coal mines, and shipping in the North brought wealth to some, and changed life for everybody. Immigrants coming from Europe went to work in factory and mine, often with small wages, long hours, and bad working conditions. Southern slave owners declared that their slaves lived better and were happier than the sweatshop workers and factory hands, including women and children, who led miserable lives in the cities of the North.

In the South, in early years, plantations were fewer, slaves were generally treated well, and planters were not striving for great wealth. The Whitney cotton gin, invented in 1794, made cotton mills important in the New England states and also in England. A race for cotton growing began in the South. More slaves were needed, their value increased, and their living conditions grew worse in many places. Slave traders made money rapidly with the increase in the demand for cotton, and while some planters had a high regard for their slaves' welfare, others were too anxious for wealth to care.

To increase production King Cotton had to have more land to the west. The Missouri Compromise had been passed in 1820 to settle the free-or-slave issue in the West, and to keep a balance between northern and southern interests in the Senate. It prohibited slavery north of the parallel 36° 30', but admitted Missouri as a slave state. At the same time the northern part of Massachusetts was admitted as the free state of Maine. This was acceptable to both the North and the South. Feeling died down for a few years.

Lincoln did not believe that slavery should be

abolished suddenly and forcibly in the South, but he knew that it must not spread north and west. During his second term in the Illinois legislature Lincoln had expressed himself publicly on the slavery issue. He and another legislator, Dan Stone, had declared they believed, on moral grounds, that slavery was both unjust and based on bad policy, but they also said they believed that the abolition doctrines would increase the evils of slavery, rather than bring about any re-form. They declared that Congress had no power to interfere with the owning of slaves in the states where slavery existed, under the Constitution, but that Congress could abolish slavery in the District of Columbia with the consent of the peo-ple there.

These were the things men talked about when-ever they gathered in stores, in taverns, in railway coaches. Whenever Mr. Lincoln came into a room all heads turned toward him, because he looked like no one else. His stories and mimicry made them laugh, and his discussion of political ques-tions made them think. As he went from court to court, defending, prosecuting, or pleading, he made more friends, and learned more about the inner workings of politics. He had some views that most of his friends did not share. He believed in giving the vote to women, and he did not believe in drinking. Nevertheless, he always refused to join groups built around these views. He wished to associate himself only with his political party.

Lincoln talked about slavery with people of many opinions. Although he did not believe in slavery, he would not join the abolitionists, or antislavery group. He discussed the slavery question with Herndon. "Why do you think that slavery should be rooted out?"

Herndon replied, "I feel it in my bones."

After that Lincoln would say that some things agreed with "Billy's bone philosophy."

There was a lot of whispered talk in every town about the "underground railroad," but nobody seemed to know who ran it, or at least they did not admit that they knew. There was a group of antislavery people in Illinois who passed runaway slaves along at night, across the river, and from house to house to freedom in Canada. "Some folks do more than talk," Lincoln heard in the streets, "they do something about it."

He knew that this was not just a question of saving a few slaves from servitude in the South— it was so big that it was likely to tear the nation apart.

The Lincoln home was on the corner of Jackson and Eighth Streets, on the edge of Springfield.

The only home Lincoln ever owned was located at Eighth and Jackson Streets in Springfield, Illinois. He bought it in 1844 (for $15,000) and lived there until becoming president.

Mr. Lincoln chopped wood for his stove and fireplaces, milked his cow and fed her every day, and put down fresh straw. Sometimes, when he came home from his round of out-of-town courts the neighbors could hear Mr. Lincoln chopping wood at midnight. The Lincolns had little interest in gardening or in raising flowers. Their story-and-a-half house was almost bare of growing things.

Mary Todd Lincoln knew that her husband was a man of an uncommon quality and she believed that he had a future. But she found that he was unable to change some of his peculiar habits, and these brought her temper flaring up. He was patient and kind, yet when a sad mood was on him he looked lost, and did not hear anything that she said to him.

As soon as Mr. Lincoln came into his home he removed his shoes, his cravat, and his coat. Then he petted the cats and kittens that were always about, and stretched out on the floor to read, with his head resting on the back of a chair laid upside down.

Mrs. Lincoln thought the little niceties of life, the social customs and manners, were important. She tried to teach her husband not to answer the door in his sockfeet, yet when the doorbell rang he forgot and padded over before the servant could get there. Lady visitors, flower-trimmed bonnets primly held on dignified heads, asked, ''Is Mrs. Lincoln at home, Mr. Lincoln?''

Mrs. Lincoln, at the top of the stairs, heard him answer, ''She'll be down as soon as she gets her trotting harness on.''

The Lincoln family was growing. After Robert came little Eddie. These children were the joy of their parents' lives. Neither father nor mother tried to restrain them much, and so they were known in the town as young terrors. When Mr. Lincoln took them to his office they overturned ink bottles, and scattered papers, until Bill Herndon in despair would leave for the day.

Life in the Lincoln home was not always pleasant, for Mrs. Lincoln's temper made it impossible to keep servant girls. The one who remained the longest was one to whom Lincoln paid extra wages in secret, saying to her with a smile, when her mistress grew angry, "Stay with her, Maria, stay with her."

Yet, for all of the household storms, these two married people were fond of each other, and knew that they each had weaknesses and that they each had strength. And always they shared their devotion for their children. Mrs. Lincoln kept house well, and moved about it as a gracious hostess, in her lovely billowing dresses.

Her husband thought that she possessed good judgment of people, and he often trusted to that. She urged him to activity, for he sometimes dropped into fits of laziness that were almost like illnesses.

Lincoln was paying up his old New Salem debts, but with the expenses of home and family he found it slow going. His law fees were small at best, and he never charged when he thought that it would be a hardship for his client to pay.

Lincoln loved children and kittens, and often stopped on the street to play with either. He never got over his fondness for a game of marbles, and could sometimes be seen crouching, a great long-legged figure of a man, over a group of small boys and a little bunch of colored marbles.

When boys knocked his high hat off one day from behind a fence, he only laughed and called, "Boys, aren't you ashamed to treat an old man like that?"

On Sundays Lincoln took his son Bob for a long walk in the country in the afternoon, or rode with both children in the old buggy behind the raw-boned horse named Buck. Sometimes he quoted poetry to them.

When a melancholy mood was on him, he repeated the poem "Mortality." This was his favorite of all poems, and the whole sadness of life seemed to him to lie in the line, "Why should the spirit of mortal be proud?" It expressed the humility that he had in his own nature.

While he felt gay he sang with them "The Blue-tail Fly," and the horse jogged along to the tune of

When I was young I used to wait,
On master and give him his plate,
And pass the bottle when he got dry,
And brush away the blue-tail fly.
Jimmie crack corn and I don't care,
My master's gone away!

Lincoln's interest in politics drew him into a race for Congress, in which his rival candidate was again old Peter Cartwright, the Methodist preacher. Lincoln traveled and spoke, and made so many friends that he began to believe that he would win the election.

One day he went to church to hear Cartwright preach. The preacher fixed his eye on Lincoln, and called for all those who did not want to go to Hell to stand. Lincoln remained seated.

"And may I inquire of you, Mr. Lincoln, where you are going?"

"If it is all the same to you, Brother Cartwright," drawled Lincoln, "I am going to Congress."

He won the election, and in the year 1847 the new congressman from Illinois, with his wife and boys, was settled in Washington.

Lincoln's life had been marked with a progress from wilderness to village, from village to town, and now from town to the capital city of the

This earliest known photograph of Lincoln was taken in 1846, just after his election to the U.S. Congress. He was 37.

United States. It was his first trip to the East. Everything was different here, and the Lincoln family had to get used to the strange ways of a community unlike their own. They lived in Mrs. Sprigg's boardinghouse where other congressmen stayed. Washington was a planned city, resting between north and south, unfinished, with the great dome of the capitol building not yet completed.

The city was like an overgrown town, where pigs roamed in the streets, and where within sound of the White House there was a busy slave market. Mrs. Lincoln found Washington unpleasant, with its mixed and moving population of congressmen, ambassadors, office hunters, and lobbyists. After a few months she took the children back to Springfield, and then to her old home in Lexington, Kentucky, for a visit.

Her husband remained at the boardinghouse, and for amusement spent some of his evenings at a nearby bowling alley, where a crowd of men always gathered about him to hear his inexhaustible fund of droll tales and stories. Before long he was known as the best storyteller in the capital.

In Congress Lincoln took a stand against the Mexican War, although the fighting was almost over by then, and annexation of Texas was a popular idea. Many people who had voted for him back in his own state were angry, and some said so in print. Lincoln knew that he would not be re-elected, and thought that when he returned to Springfield at the end of the term he would be out of politics for good. When his elected term was over he went back to his law practice and continued traveling by horseback or carriage, on the circuit that carried him through fourteen counties.

The flow and movement of life was changing. In 1849 the discovery of gold in California brought men in a great rush across the western plains and mountains, going westward, always westward. Then came the settlement of Oregon, by people hungry for good land of their own. The states of Indiana and Illinois were no longer the western frontier. Cities sprang up rapidly and farmers got better machinery and grew larger crops.

Now railroads were stretching their iron tracks from city to city, and rivers no longer were so important to trade. The eyes and the interests of the people of Illinois turned away from the broad Mississippi and the Southland, to the north-eastern states. Railroads were drawing them closer to New York, Philadelphia, and Boston. Railroads were making the town of Chicago a vast city. For a few years people were so busy con-structing towns and cities, factories, railroads, and canals that they thought less of the slavery question.

Then, in 1850, the burning question of whether new states in the West should be free or slave again became an angry issue splitting the country. In 1845 Texas had been admitted as a slave state, but California, which had been ceded to the United States along with New Mexico at the end of the Mexican War in 1848, prohibited slavery as soon as its state government was formed.

In the Senate Henry Clay proposed a compromise that he hoped would preserve the Union. This compromise admitted California as a free state, but permitted the territories of Utah and New Mexico to be established without determining whether they should be slaveholding or free. The District of Columbia was to have a prohibition of the slave trade, though not of slavery. The North was rapidly growing stronger than the South, and the voting balance in the Senate was now in its favor, but the South was pleased by the passage of a federal law returning fugitive slaves. Then for four years the slavery issue, as it affected the admission of new states, grew less important.

Lincoln was out of politics, but as he rode in his old black buggy behind his horse Buck from town to town on his lawyer's circuit, his thoughts were dwelling on the political problems and the tense issues of the day. The explosive slavery question had not been settled, but was only resting for a while, not far beneath the surface of American life. It was opened up again by a short, persuasive man called the "Little Giant." This was Stephen A. Douglas, already known to Lincoln in Illinois. Douglas was a senator, chairman of the Senate committee on territories, and he wished to promote a plan to build the transcontinental railroad along a northern route in the West. This was opposed by the South, for the western country through which it would run would not be slave states.

In 1854 Douglas put through Congress his Kansas-Nebraska bill, which would allow popular sovereignty, or the right of the people to decide in the new territories whether they wished slavery or not, and repeal the Missouri Compromise. The passage of this bill whipped up a storm of angry criticism in the North.

When Lincoln heard of the repeal of the Compromise he said that he was roused as never before. He went back into politics and began to make speeches to help re-elect a friend, Richard Yates, to Congress. When Douglas came to Springfield to speak in defense of the Kansas-Nebraska bill, Lincoln answered him publicly the next day. Lincoln said that the South had a Constitutional right to slavery, but that slavery should not be extended into new territories. The speech made a good impression on his audience, and was talked about throughout the state. In spite of this, however, Douglas was re-elected, and Lincoln realized that a new combination of political forces was necessary to uphold this issue. He joined the new party called Republican.

The Republicans, at the beginning, were mainly abolitionists and other uncompromising extremists. But with the Kansas-Nebraska issue assuming importance, the political parties began to change. Forces against the repeal of the Compromise act came together, and the Whig party finally went out of existence. In May of 1854 Lincoln made a speech in Bloomington, Illinois, where the first official Republican convention was held. His partner, Herndon, declared that this was the greatest speech of the many ever delivered by Lincoln. It became known as the ''lost speech,'' for the audience was so absorbed and excited that nobody remembered to takes notes on it.

Then, in 1857, came the famous Dred Scott case, when a black man, who had been freed in a non-slave territory, went back to a slave state and was declared a slave again. This decision, that a slave was not a citizen, but was property, was rendered by Supreme Court Justice Taney. This meant that if a slaveowner took his slave into a free territory, then the slave could not be taken from him, even if the territory were free by law. If this was true Congress could not prohibit slavery in the territories.

Writers and speakers in New England made a moral crusade of it. William Lloyd Garrison cried in his *Liberator*, ''No Union with slaveholders!'' and secession meetings were held in many places in the North. A feeling that secession was the only answer to these questions was growing both in the North and in the South. Douglas was speaking his views, and so was Lincoln, on the burning issues of the day.

Douglas defended the Dred Scott decision, while Lincoln opposed it. Lincoln declared that it would be hard to find many owners who would send a slave back to freedom in Africa, as some thought should be done, when this kind of live ''property'' could be sold for fifteen hundred dollars in Kansas.

The people who wanted to do away with slavery entirely and suddenly were not so many in numbers, but they were filled with anger and were able to make themselves heard. There were orators, preachers, poets, and prose writers—

Lincoln called this photograph, taken in February 1857 at the age of 48, "a very true one."

such as Whittier, Emerson, Lowell, Beecher, Whitman, and Harriet Beecher Stowe. Everybody talked about Kansas, and called it "Bloody Kansas." Was Kansas to be a slave state, or a free one? A tall bearded man named John Brown was carrying on a private war of his own with slaveowners, and was stealing horses, killing people, and running slaves to freedom. In Kansas civil war broke out, with feeling running high. Lincoln said of Kansas, "If you have the majority, as some of you say you have, you can succeed with the ballot, throwing away the bullet. Let there be peace."

It was hard to be reasonable about Kansas, though, when men, women, and children were being killed by both sides, and homes burned. Anger flared high in the North when the news spread that the governor of Kansas, an antislavery man, had been captured by a slaveholding crowd and tied out on the prairie while his home was burned. Lincoln knew the South lived in constant fear of slave uprisings that might come with a sudden removal of restraints, and also that they feared the ruin of their economy. Yet he knew that slavery was wrong, and he believed that sooner or later the issue would have to be settled.

The Bloomington speech had attracted so much attention that Lincoln was offered the opportunity to run for the Senate against the "Little Giant," Stephen A. Douglas. In May, 1858, Abraham Lincoln delivered the speech that he later declared was the one thing on his record he would wish to remain if all else had to be destroyed. In accepting the nomination for the Senate he said, "A house divided against itself cannot stand. I believe this government cannot endure, permanently, half slave and half free."

Douglas rejoiced at this, for he felt that this speech insured the success of his race against Lincoln. He said that Lincoln was an able and an honest man, but he thought that this statement called for war between the slave and non-slave states. Lincoln challenged the "Little Giant" to a series of seven debates that became the most celebrated in the history of the country.

People talked excitedly of this contest. They came to hear the speeches on horseback, in carriages, by train, and on foot. They brought brass bands, marched in processions, waved flags, and shouted. With each debate, discussion grew louder and excitement spread farther.

In the first debate Lincoln asked whether people of a territory could exclude slavery before being admitted as a state. Douglas said that it was up to the people of a territory to have slavery or not, and that slavery could be kept out by legislation to that effect, in the territory. Slavery was always the issue. Lincoln stated again that he had no wish to interfere in the slave states, but he wanted to turn back the trend toward spreading slavery, and that he felt that if the people of the country would believe that slavery would disappear finally the Union would be safe.

At Quincy he said: "Because we think it wrong, we propose a course of policy that shall deal with it as wrong. We deal with it as with any other wrong, in so far as we can prevent its growing any larger, and so deal with it that in the run of time there may be some promise of an end to it."

In places where most people believed in slavery Douglas was popular, but in the antislavery towns people cheered Lincoln. Douglas rode in a private railroad car, while Lincoln often came as a passenger in a day coach on the same train. Once he arrived in a boxcar, when he hadn't been able to catch the passenger train. All over the North readers fixed their eyes on Lincoln's printed speeches when they read their newspapers, and asked, "Just who is this western countryman, that he can talk and write with such deep understanding and knowledge?"

They also said, in some places, "These are the greatest speeches ever made in this country."

In 1858, Lincoln held seven debates with his opponent for the U.S. Senate, Stephen A. Douglas (seated to Lincoln's right). Although Douglas won reelection, Lincoln's powerful arguments against slavery made him a prominent figure.

The preparation of these debates made Lincoln think carefully and clarify his views. They brought him to a decision: that this nation should not be divided, and that the Union was greater than any state alone. When the voting was over Lincoln found that he had a popular majority, but that Douglas had won. Lincoln had lost the Senate election, yet these debates made him known to the country, both North and South.

When asked how he felt about his defeat he remarked, "It was like the little boy who stubbed his toe. It hurt too bad to laugh, and he was too big to cry."

Once more lawyer Lincoln went back to his law practice, jogging about the countryside with his stovepipe hat full of papers, his rusty black umbrella over his arm, and his gray woolen shawl pulled across his shoulders in chilly weather. Then came a law case involving old friends. Jack Armstrong, of Clary's Grove, had died only a short time after his son Duff had got into serious trouble. Jack's wife Hannah came to her friend Mr. Lincoln to ask him to help her son.

He gathered his things together and rode to Beardstown to defend Duff Armstrong against a charge of murder. A man named Metzker had died as the result of a drunken fight, and a witness told the jury that in bright moonlight he had seen the victim hit by a slingshot held by Duff Armstrong.

Hannah Armstrong watched, in tears, and listened to Lincoln as he spoke. He told of the friendship that she and her husband had shown a penniless youth in the years in New Salem, and he said that these were good people. Then Lincoln slowly opened an almanac, and showed that on the night of the fight the moon had not given enough light to allow a witness to see, at the time stated, such an act as a blow with a slingshot. Duff Armstrong was cleared of the murder charge, while the folk in the courtroom laughed and cheered. They said that Mr. Lincoln was a pretty smart man—smart enough for any job.

The home on Jackson and Eighth Streets had grown larger with the years, and changes had taken place in it. Mrs. Lincoln had had the house remodeled by adding a second story. She had a great liking for fine house furnishings, a liking not shared by her husband, who never seemed to notice his surroundings. He did not make a big income as a lawyer, and he had been obliged to pay off a debt over the years. Mary knew that he disapproved of her extravagance, but she spent money anyway, and could never resist the urge to buy, even if doing so meant debts followed by quarrels. As the years passed she failed to learn any self-control in regard to money, and every sad or unpleasant event in her life seemed to bring on more frequent outbursts of hysteria.

During the winter of 1850 sorrow had come to the Lincoln home, for four-year-old Edward had become seriously ill. Mary and Abraham loved their children devotedly, and when Edward died they were overcome with grief. Then in the autumn of that year another boy was born to them. He was the brightest of all of the Lincoln children—the one most like his father in mind and spirit. His name was William. The fourth son, Thomas, called Tad, was born three years later. Tad was a lively child, who had an impediment in his speech and possessed the quick, attractive, and tempestuous disposition of his mother. The house was noisy with the antics of the three children, and, no matter how mischievous they became, their father and mother could seldom bring themselves to punish them.

Mr. Lincoln was busy during these years. His travels on the circuit, visiting many courthouses, seeing many people, were important to him. They kept him in touch with the lives, the thoughts, and the hopes of the people. He was away a good deal of the time, sleeping in inns and hotel rooms, eating in restaurants or with friends.

Knowledge of events in the nation came to the lawyer from talk, argument, and from reading newspapers as he traveled about. In 1851 an energetic little woman called Harriet Beecher Stowe had published a book that seemed to set the country on fire. It was *Uncle Tom's Cabin, or Life Among the Lowly*. Although she had little first-hand knowledge of Southern conditions, Mrs. Stowe had written a book so packed with anti-slavery feeling that the sales soon reached more than three hundred thousand, and it was read in many other countries and languages.

In 1859 John Brown, the violent abolitionist, with seventeen other men, came from Kansas to attack and capture a government arsenal at Harpers Ferry, Virginia, declaring that the slaves were free. After Colonel Robert E. Lee and a detachment of marines recaptured the building John Brown was tried and condemned to death by hanging. When friends wanted to try to rescue him from jail, he refused, saying that he would be more useful to the antislavery cause dead than alive. He was right, for the extreme abolitionists John Brown was a martyr.

While the antislavery group fanned the flame of feeling higher and southern feeling rose with it, Lincoln was sitting in his dusty office, feet on table, gazing out of the window, thinking. He thought of his own future, and of the tremendous questions of the times. When asked whether he wanted to take part in politics, perhaps run for president, he said, ''The taste for it is in my mouth a little.'' By 1859 he was ready to be a candidate for the Republican nomination for president.

In February, 1860, Lincoln went to New York City, where he delivered a speech at Cooper Union, sponsored by the Young Men's Central Republican Union. He was introduced by the poet William Cullen Bryant. In the audience there were many easterners who were surprised at first sight of the tall, gawky, and yet impressive man, and they listened with complete attention as he began to speak.

He talked of the Constitution of the United States, and stated that the makers of it had never intended to allow slavery to spread. As for John Brown's raid at Harpers Ferry, Lincoln said: "John Brown was no Republican; and you have failed to implicate a single Republican in his Harpers Ferry enterprise. John Brown's effort was peculiar. It was an effort by white men to get up a revolt among slaves, in which the slaves refused to participate. In fact, it was so absurd that the slaves, with all their ignorance, saw plainly enough it could not succeed."

He continued, "What will satisfy the South? Simply this: we must not only let them alone, but we must somehow convince them that we do let them alone."

Lincoln finished with a declaration that slavery must be prevented, with the vote, from spreading into territories and free states. "If our sense of duty forbids this, then let us stand by our duty, fearlessly and effectively."

As he went out into a snowstorm, and returned to the Astor House by streetcar, the applause of the enthusiastic crowd rang in his ears. Yes, the taste of politics was in his mouth, and would remain there. From New York he went to see his son Robert, who was in school in New Hampshire, and then made several speeches in New England. All this was leading up to the Republican Convention, to be held in fast-growing, sprawling Chicago.

In May, 1860, the state convention met in Decatur, Illinois, to choose a candidate for the national convention. Lincoln's friends wanted a slogan to set the thought of their candidate in people's heads.

They called Lincoln the "rail-splitter" candidate, and had his old friend and cousin, John Hanks, march into the hall with a banner nailed to rails that Hanks declared he and Abe had split many years ago. Lincoln smiled when he saw the rails, drew in his lips thoughtfully as he looked them over, and then said, "I cannot say that I split these rails. They are honey locust and walnut; that is lasting timber. It may be that I split these rails. Well, boys, I can only say that I have split a great many better-looking ones."

Later in the same month, Lincoln became known to the Republican Convention in Chicago as "The Rail Candidate," or "The Rail Splitter."

The convention assembled in June in a new

building in Chicago called "The Wigwam," but Lincoln did not go. He knew that Senator William Seward was the popular candidate, although there were others running, too. At home in Springfield Lincoln received excited telegrams, telling him which way the voting was going. One wire said that a certain Cameron delegation could be had if promised the Treasury Department. Lincoln wired back: I AUTHORIZE NO BARGAINS AND WILL BE BOUND BY NONE.

During the day the tall man in the stovepipe hat wandered around Springfield, showing no signs of restlessness, but still unable to sit in his office to wait for final voting returns. He went to his home, to his office, to the bowling alley, and then out to the square to talk to farmers hitching their horses in front of stores.

At noon on Friday, when Lincoln was in the office of the newspaper, a man ran through the dusty streets and into the room where Lincoln was, to thrust a telegram into his hands. He unfolded it, and read slowly. It told him that Abraham Lincoln was the Republican candidate for President of the United States.

Suddenly a crowd was around him, people were shouting the news, and he was shaking hands with everybody. His wide mouth creased in a smile. He said, "I reckon there's a little short

In June 1860 (when this photograph was taken), Lincoln won the Republican Party nomination for president.

woman down at our house that is more interested in this news than I am.''

That night bonfires burned in celebration throughout southern Illinois. People gathered around the house of the Lincoln family to shout and sing until dawn. Parades marched with torches flaring, and barrels of burning tar flamed high. The sound of voices rose and fell all night in Springfield.

> Old Abe came out of the wilderness,
> Out of the wilderness, down in Illinois.

They shouted for Honest Abe, Old Abe, and for the Rail Candidate.

Next day neighbors came in to help make preparations for the arrival of the official committee from Chicago. Political friends offered to bring whisky and beer to serve the guests, but Lincoln thanked them and said no. When the committee from Chicago arrived to make the official announcement to Lincoln, their host offered cold water, saying, ''Gentlemen, let us drink to our mutual good health in this wholesome drink which God has given us. It is the only drink I permit my family, and in all conscience let me not depart from this custom on this occasion.''

The struggle for the presidency in this crucial year was hot with words, furious with many feelings. In the South the news of the Republican choice lighted a fire of rebellion. If Abraham Lincoln was to be President, many declared, southern states would secede.

Lincoln established headquarters in the capitol building in Springfield, and there he spent every day greeting friends and well-wishers. They came in crowds—country men and women in rawhide boots and homespun clothing, in calico dresses and sunbonnets, distinguished men from the East and West, Horace Greeley, famous editor of the New York *Tribune*, and Carl Schurz, German newspaperman from Wisconsin. They came to the house, too, where Willie and Tad ran around in great excitement among the important visitors.

Republicans knew that they had a good chance to win the election, for the Democrats had split between South and West. Stephen A. Douglas received the backing of the western group, but the southerners walked out of the convention and nominated John C. Breckinridge.

On election night Mr. Lincoln went to the telegraph office to watch the returns, while outside in the streets crowds moved and shouted and sang. When the final word came, the President-elect seemed less excited than any man there. He had carried all of the states in the North except one. He spent most of the night at home shaking hands with everybody who came, smiling at the greeting, ''Congratulations, Mr. President.''

Across the western plains and mountains news of the election of Abraham Lincoln was carried to California by the pounding riders of the Pony Express.

A little girl wrote to ask Mr. Lincoln why he did not wear a beard. This suggestion met his approval, and after the election he started to grow a beard. Mrs. Lincoln traveled to New York to buy fine dresses for Washington society, while her husband took a trip to see his old stepmother. Tom Lincoln was dead, but Sarah Bush Lincoln gave Abe a hug and did not seem surprised at the news. To be elected President of the United States was no more than she would have expected of Abraham.

Then Mr. Lincoln returned to write his inaugural speech, to sell his furniture and rent his house. On his last day in Springfield, Lincoln said to his law partner Billy Herndon, ''Let our sign hang there. If I live I'm coming back to practice law again.''

Early in the morning of February 11, 1861, Lincoln stood in a misty rain on the rear platform of his train. He was dressed in black broadcloth, as usual, and wore a woolen shawl over his high shoulders. A crowd of old friends, fellow towns-men and countrymen waited quietly in the rain as Mr. Lincoln spoke:

> My friends, no one not in my situation can appreci-ate my feeling of sadness at this parting. To this place, and the kindness of these people I owe ev-erything. Here I have lived a quarter of a century and have passed from a young to an old man. Here my children have been born, and one is buried. I now leave, not knowing when, or whether ever, I may return, with a task before me greater than that which rested upon Washington. Without the assist-ance of that Divine Being who ever attended him, I cannot succeed. With that assistance I cannot fail. Trusting in Him who can go with me, and remain with you and be everywhere for good, let us con-fidently hope that all will yet be well. To His care commending you, as I hope in your prayers you will commend me, I bid you an affectionate farewell.

The train whistle blew a shrill blast, the con-ductor shouted, "All aboard." Bells rang and the little diamond-stack locomotive pulled out with the presidential party, accompanied by Mrs. Lin-coln and the boys, in the one car for passengers. The tall gaunt man in his high stovepipe hat stood looking silently at the city of Springfield, and the brown prairies of Illinois, as they disappeared from his sight.

The journey to Washington was a slow one, with speeches at several towns along the way. In Philadelphia Lincoln was to speak at the raising of the flag of the newly admitted state of Kansas. There he was told by his friend Norman Judd and a detective, Allan Pinkerton, that enemies were planning to kill him as he passed through Baltimore. Although he did not believe this, the President-elect thought it best not to ignore the urgent requests for safety presented by his advisers, and so changed quietly to another train in Harrisburg. With a friend, Ward Hill Lamon, Lincoln traveled to Washington through Baltimore dressed in borrowed clothing, and an old cap instead of the well-known tall hat.

March 4 was filled with wild rumors that Lincoln would be shot before he could take office, but on this windy inauguration day in 1861, when the sky was an uncertain mass of moving clouds and sudden flashes of lightning quivered, Mr. Lincoln put on his spectacles and read his message.

He would not compromise with the principle that the Union must be preserved. As he stood on the platform the problem of secession and of Fort Sumter was in everyone's thoughts. Already seven southern states had seceded from the Union and formed a Confederate government.

Fort Sumter, on an island in the harbor of Charleston, South Carolina—a state that had seceded—was part of the federal defenses of the country, and was held by government troops. They needed supplies immediately, and if they received them, and held the fort, the war might start there.

The new President pledged himself to uphold the Constitution and to enforce the laws of the land. Then he appealed to the southern states, saying: ''You can have no conflict, without being yourselves the aggressors. You have no oath registered in Heaven to destroy the government, while I shall have the most solemn one to 'preserve, protect, and defend it.' ''

Abraham Lincoln was sworn in as President of the United States, and went home to the White House. Mary Lincoln found her new home in a condition of shabbiness and disrepair. Nothing could please her more than the opportunity to refurnish and redecorate it, and so she was delighted when she heard that Congress had appropriated $20,000 for this purpose. While her husband struggled with the vital and dangerous problems confronting him, and at the same time tried to get used to swarms of office seekers that troubled him, Mrs. Lincoln was buying new carpets and silk curtains and furniture in Philadelphia and New York. She furnished the White House with beauty and good taste, but in doing so ran over her allotted sum of money. When Lincoln heard of it he was angry, and called her down sharply for spending so much money on house furnishings. Congress, however, passed a bill to take care of the deficit.

The First Lady of the land had the quality and the education for her position as hostess in the White House, but her sharp tongue turned friends away. She had few intimates, and was much criticized. Mr. Lincoln never turned anyone away. He made time for every request, every plea and every complaint. Crowds of men and women came daily to the White House, and he saw them all until he was weary, and could scarcely shake another hand. Office seekers were especially bothersome, asking for favors.

He soon formed a habit of going to the War Department, where he often sat in the telegraph room reading or working. Here he could get away from strangers. He had to make a most difficult decision—whether to relieve Fort Sumter or to allow it to be taken by the Confederates. After much anxious thought he decided to send a ship with food supplies.

On April 12, 1861, before the relief ship reached it, Fort Sumter was fired on by Confederate batteries. The fort surrendered after a period of fighting that lasted a day and a half. Now, unless the other six southern states remained in the Union war could not be prevented. People of all shades of political opinion in the capital came to assure Lincoln of their support—for the whole country was tense with the realization that the United States was about to be plunged into a devastating civil war.

Even so, most people did not believe that war would last long. In the North people talked in country stores, and on street corners in towns, saying, "Well, if war comes it won't last more than a few weeks." In the secession states young men boasted, "We'll have the Yankees licked in a month, or before." But older men in the South looked grave, and said little, for many of them understood better what was ahead, and many did not want division of the Union.

On April 14, Lincoln conferred with his cabinet and talked with his old rival, Stephen A. Douglas. Douglas issued a statement saying that although he disagreed with Lincoln politically he would support him completely in any effort to preserve the Union. Next day Lincoln called for 75,000 militiamen to sign up for a period of three months.

In the South this touched off the explosion.

Most southerners felt more loyalty to their own states than to the country as a whole. Freedom to them meant freedom for their home states to follow their chosen way of life, while in the North freedom meant preservation of the Union.

Four of the remaining southern states seceded—Virginia, North Carolina, Arkansas, and Tennessee. It was uncertain for some time whether Kentucky and Maryland would join the Confederacy, and Lincoln was in great anxiety about them. Missouri was also a state where people were divided in their loyalty. Lincoln made every effort to keep the border slave states from seceding, and managed to do so. Delaware was a slave state that did not leave the Union.

Alexander Stevens, a Georgia statesman who had not so long before made a speech in which he said that he was not in favor of breaking the Union, now joined the Confederacy. He stated, ''We fight for our homes, our fathers and mothers, brothers, sisters, sons and daughters.'' Robert Toombs of Georgia, a friend of Lincoln's in Congress, who had also not wanted secession, now declared for it, and became the Confederate Secretary of State.

Colonel Robert E. Lee, of Virginia, was called to Washington April 18 by old General Winfield

Scott. Lee had previously said, "If the Union is dissolved and the government disrupted, I shall return to my native state and share the miseries of my people and save in defense will draw my sword on none." Now he answered the offer of command of the United States forces by this reply, "Though opposed to secession and deprecating war, I can take no part in an invasion of the Southern States." Instead, he accepted the post of commanding general of the Confederate army. Scott and Lincoln both knew that Lee was the best officer in the United States army.

In the terrible days that followed families and friends, separated by different loyalties, became enemies. In the border states some went into the Union army and some into the Confederate. Washington was in a dangerous position, just across the Potomac from Virginia. In the capital city itself there were many who sided with the South.

As spring came to Washington and leaves budded on the trees along Pennsylvania Avenue, the war took over the city. This broad avenue was filled with horses, carriages of congressmen and senators, hacks, horse-drawn streetcars, bands, and marching troops. Soldiers rode through throngs of people from the frontiers, as well as from the eastern states, New York and New England, Indians, blacks, and foreign immigrants just arrived from Europe.

Washington suddenly outgrew its housing, its sleepy southern air, and its traditions. Buildings rose rapidly, with the noise of hammer and saw, and the scent of magnolia blossoms seemed out of place now in the dust and din.

The first battle took place on Bull Run at Manassas, Virginia. The President stood at a window, with his hands clasped behind his back, and watched silently as troops marched through the city, flags flying, bands playing. Then he saw men and women, dressed in their best as if on the way to a festival, riding out in carriages to witness the battle. Later from the War Department he also saw their panicky return to the city after the defeat of the northern forces. That night Mr. Lincoln did not go to bed at all; striding back and forth all night, he read reports of the disastrous battle.

The wounded were brought into the city, in the first of many wagons and ambulances from the battlefields, winding slowly through the streets to hospitals.

Demands on the President and his wife were numerous, and social life presented problems. Even with the country torn apart in a life-and-death struggle, Washington tradition required the

President and his wife to entertain. Mr. and Mrs. Lincoln thought it more appropriate to the times to discontinue some of the large state dinners and hold receptions instead. Men and women came in great numbers.

Mr. Lincoln, with the unfailing courtesy and easy manner that had always made friends for him, shook hands until his gloves were soiled, and sometimes burst at the seams. Then, when the guests had left, he went with his lively boys to see the new kittens and puppies, and laugh and romp with them. In the late afternoon he sometimes took a drive with his wife, and at night went back to his duties as President and Commander-in-Chief of the army. After dark he could be seen strolling across to the War Department.

From the beginning of the war the army command was the most difficult problem that Lincoln had to solve. The South had always sent young men to West Point, and the military tradition of the planters' sons produced fine officers, who were not only able but also possessed great spirit. They were now in the Confederate army. General Scott was not well, and was too old to fight in the field. General McClellan was put in command of the Army of the Potomac. He was an able officer, and a good organizer, but uncertain and overcautious. Lincoln was bombarded with criticisms of McClellan as time passed, for people said he was so arrogant that he considered himself another Napoleon. Lincoln refused to allow personal arrogance to affect his decisions, but he could not overlook the fact that McClellan was not the man to lead an army successfully against General Lee, who proved to be a genius in military tactics.

The war went badly for the Union forces during the first two years. Lee was not the only brilliant officer in the Confederate army, for Stonewall Jackson was a rocky barrier to northern success, and the skill of General Joseph E. Johnston and the dash and daring of Jeb Stuart and others won battles. In the North young men from farms and cities joined to fight for the principle of freedom as they saw it, and for the preservation of the Union. In the South hotheaded planters' sons faced fire in defense of their belief in slavery and states' rights, but boys from farms and villages in the South put on the gray uniform of the Confederate army to fight for their homes. The South believed, as Lee did, that the war was against invasion.

Lincoln endured a vast ebb and flow of praise and blame during the first two years. Trying to find a commander who would attack and keep attacking successfully, he shifted command from McClellan to Burnside and to Hooker, and back to McClellan. During this period in Lincoln's life he moved from a position in which he often felt undecided and ignorant of military affairs, to one of confidence and knowledge that made him the real commander-in-chief of the Union army. He still made his decisions slowly, but he made them forcefully, and never backed down under criticism. He came to understand that not one but many reasons were behind the secession of the South, and that the most important one was that the South wanted to govern itself and protect its own way of life, which was different from that of the North. He learned that the South would not give up, and would have to be defeated on the battlefields to end the war.

During these years Lincoln also became a great writer. He avoided the typical fancy speech of the day, and placed his thoughts in clear, simple, and noble language. His favorite books were still Burns, Shakespeare, and the Bible. He also liked the humor of plain, homely people, and enjoyed reading it to others. Sometimes as his two secretaries worked late at night they would be startled to see the President come walking into their office in his nightshirt to read them a funny story.

His chief pleasure was watching the happy

antics of his two small boys. Willie and Tad made
a great playhouse of the official mansion. They
put on shows in the attic, and played on the roof,
and sent the place into an uproar when they
yanked on the bell cords, bringing the servants
running. The Taft children, Bud and Holly, often
joined in the fun, riding the pony and frolicking
with the goat. Once when the boys delivered a
death sentence to a soldier doll, their father solemnly issued a pardon, which read: "The doll
Jack is pardoned. By order of the President. A.
Lincoln."

In February of 1862 Willie developed a fever,
and became seriously ill. Mary and Abraham Lincoln watched him in great anxiety, and were relieved to receive an encouraging report from the
doctor. Then on an evening when the White
House was filled with guests attending a reception arranged some time before, the parents were
told that Willie was suddenly worse. After that
they spent even more hours at his bedside, and
also with Tad, who was ill now too. On February
20 Willie died, and Lincoln, whose face was lined
with sorrow, had to put his feelings aside because
of his concern for his wife and for Tad.

Tad gradually improved, and was soon on the
road to recovery, but Mary Lincoln was almost out
of her mind with grief. Her husband knew that

her nerves could not cope with the strains put upon them. She was blamed in the South for being a traitor to her home and her own family, since her brother-in-law and her two half brothers were in the Confederate army. And in the North she was accused of being in sympathy with the South, and was called a "Copperhead," which was the contemptuous name given southern sympathizers and spies. Her health was not good, and the loss of Willie was a serious threat to her reason.

As she recovered her health, however, Mary Lincoln pleased her husband greatly by spending much of her time visiting the hospitals and doing all that she could for the sick and wounded. Lincoln kept Tad beside him a great deal. Tad wore a blue uniform that was a small duplicate of an officer's in the Union army. He rode beside the tall figure of the President on parade, and he often sat with Lincoln, even when his father was in the midst of an important conference.

Lincoln made decisions that sometimes brought violent reactions against him. Early in the war he had appointed popular John C. Frémont to command the forces in the West, but had relieved him of his post when Frémont rashly, and without consulting the President, sent out an order to free the slaves in Missouri. This action on the part of Lincoln brought a storm of protest in the press.

He was no less criticized in another matter. When two diplomats were sent to England by the Confederacy, and were taken from a British ship and returned to the United States by the American captain who had removed them, the North rejoiced. Lincoln, however, knew that there was a great deal of sympathy for the Confederacy in upper classes in England, and that to hold these men might bring on war with Great Britain. He had the Confederate ambassadors released, and allowed them to go on to England. When he was berated for this, Lincoln said, with a wry smile, "One war at a time."

A new danger appeared on the sea, for the old wooden ship, the *Merrimac*, had been sheathed with iron plates and sent out to do considerable damage to Union ships surprised in Chesapeake Bay. With astonishing speed a vessel called the *Monitor* was launched against the *Merrimac*. She was built with an iron bottom, iron turret, and iron decks. People said that the *Monitor* looked like a cheese box on a raft, but she defeated the *Merrimac*. The *Monitor* and the *Merrimac* proved that ironclad vessels, however old and makeshift, were superior in combat to wooden fighting ships.

Lincoln went often to the White House roof to gaze at the Potomac through his spyglass. His thoughts never left the war for long, even when he strolled to the stables with Tad and laughed to see the pet goat, Nanka, chasing the groom.

Petitioners came every day. A mother pleaded for her son, who had fallen asleep on guard duty, and been condemned to be shot. Lincoln issued pardons wherever he could do so. Sometimes there were wives, wanting desperately to go to husbands ill in hospitals in the South, and he gave them passes. There were old friends from Illinois asking for jobs. One day passers-by were surprised to see the President sitting on the curb near the War Department writing a pass for a woman who stood waiting.

A pass to the battle lines was also given to Matthew Brady, the first photographer ever to take pictures of a war. And then, later, the President looked for a long time at these photographs of men in wrinkled, dirty uniforms, on the desolated battlefields. Men were fighting gallantly on both sides. When firing let up, and they had the opportunity, they swapped tobacco and talked and joked before going back to their guns. Officers of both armies were known to each other, and often were old friends, having attended West Point together. Lincoln searched for commanding

In early October 1862, shortly after the Battle of Antietam, President Lincoln visited the war front. With him are Secret Service Chief Allan Pinkerton (left) and Major General John A. McClernand (right). The photo was taken by Mathew Brady.

officers who could end the war with victory. The North had the advantage in man power, in sea power, and in supplies from factories and mines. But the South was fighting on home territory among fiercely sympathetic civilians.

News was as gloomy as the black storm clouds that sometimes swept in from the ocean over the noisy, crowded city of Washington. Battles were lost in Virginia—in the Wilderness, at Fredericksburg, around Richmond and Yorktown. Along the cobbles of Pennsylvania Avenue pounded the feet of regiments marching south, singing a new song written by Julia Ward Howe, to the tune of "John Brown's Body." Soldiers in blue sang this "Battle Hymn of the Republic" as they marched to Tennessee and to Virginia. Soldiers in gray sang "Dixie" as they came up the dusty roads and rode the railroad cars, from Florida and Georgia, and from distant Texas.

Some men and women demanded constantly, in newspapers and in speeches, freedom for the slaves. President Lincoln thought long on this. He had believed that it should be left to states to free their own slaves, and that this would come to pass in time. But spreading slavery into other states and territories was another matter. Even as he considered a proclamation of emancipation for slaves he answered Greeley, of the New York

Tribune, who had said that the President failed in his duty by not freeing all slaves.

> My object in this struggle is to save the Union, and is not either to save or destroy slavery. If I could save the Union without freeing any slaves I would do it, and if I could save it by freeing all the slaves I would do it; and if I could save it by freeing some and leaving others alone I would also do that. I shall try to correct errors when shown to be errors; and I shall adopt new views so fast as they shall appear to be true views. I have here stated my purpose according to my view of official duty, and I intend no modification of my oft-expressed personal wish that all men everywhere could be free.

Yet Lincoln still believed that "a nation half slave, and half free, could not long survive." He came to the conclusion that the war could not be won without freedom for the slaves. This was a necessity for political and military reasons. The army of the North was embarrassed by hordes of blacks who came to their camps, and officers were asking for black troops. Politically, emancipation would strengthen the northern cause, for the people of England and France did not believe in slavery. Economically, the move would aid the winning of the war, for with the slaves free the South would not have a dependable fund of labor.

During the hot summer months as the President sat in the telegraph office in the War Department, he stared at the motionless dusty leaves on the trees, and he wrote slowly, a sentence at a time. In his ears were the tapping of the telegraph instruments, and the hum of voices on the street outside. Mr. Lincoln was writing the Emancipation Proclamation, the order that would end slavery in the United States. He took his time, and even after it was written in the summer of 1862, he held it back, on the advice of his cabinet, until the Union had won a victory at Antietam.

On New Year's Day, 1863, the proclamation went into effect, and when news of it reached the South there was anger and fear among white people and singing and rejoicing among slaves. In the North some were enthusiastic, others critical, thinking it not strong enough, and still others resentful, for they said that Lincoln had gone back on his own belief that the war was not to free slaves, but only to preserve the Union.

Wrinkles in the President's brow deepened as the war went on. Time after time his generals failed to counterattack quickly, or they withdrew their armies at the moment when that meant defeat. Lincoln wanted a man who would attack, and continue to attack.

Then came the battle of Gettysburg. Lincoln sat all day in his office, his head heavy with fatigue. Lee had brought his army into Pennsyl-

vania and had met General Meade, who had suc-
ceeded Hooker, at Gettysburg. This was the most
frightful battle of the war. For three days both
sides suffered terrible losses on the grassy fields
and wooded hillsides, which became the scene of
heroic charges. Lee lost, and withdrew his army
back across the Potomac, and Meade did not pur-
sue him.

Lincoln read the battle reports over and over as
he listened to public rejoicing at the victory. He
knew that the war would not end while his generals refused, or were unable, to follow up the
Confederate forces.

From the Mississippi region the President received news of victories in Tennessee. He studied
reports from General Ulysses Grant and knew
him to be a bulldog sort of a man, who did not let
go. As Lincoln read the reports, sitting at his desk
night after night, where he worked late to avoid
the throngs of people in the White House by day,
he decided to watch Grant closely. There were
advisers opposed to Grant, and Mrs. Lincoln told
him that people called Grant a "butcher" and
said that he had more regard for his horses than
for his men. Yet Lincoln knew that General Grant
was a very able commander, and one with a re-
lentless drive. Lincoln said quietly, "I can't spare
this man. He fights."

The dead on the battlefield of Gettysburg had been buried where they fell, blue and gray uniforms together. A move that was made to have them reburied, and graves marked, resulted in the founding of a National Cemetery. The dedication ceremony was held there October 23, 1863.

Edward Everett, a well-known orator, was invited to deliver the principal speech, and President Lincoln was asked to say a few words. He wrote a brief speech just before he boarded the train, and made his revisions on it as the rattling cars carried him to Gettysburg. At ten o'clock in the morning a band played as it escorted the procession to the cemetery. Lincoln rode, tall and serious in his black clothing and high silk hat. Everett was a master of oratory, and he spoke for two hours to a large crowd that liked elaborate speaking. When he finished and sat down to loud applause, the short speech of the President could scarcely come as anything but an anticlimax. Lincoln rose and stepped forward. He adjusted his spectacles carefully, looked over his two sheets of paper, and began to speak.

People had already heard enough oratory, and their attention wandered. They did not really take in the speech at all. There was only a spattering of applause as Lincoln finished. The President looked disturbed, and when he returned to his train after a reception that tired him, he stretched out on a seat with a wet towel on his head and said to Ward Hill Lamon, ''I tell you, Hill, that speech fell on the audience like a wet blanket. I am distressed about it. I ought to have prepared it with more care.''

When he returned to the White House he felt ill, and his doctor found that he was suffering from a mild case of smallpox. Lincoln laughed when told of this, and said, listening to the voices of petitioners downstairs, ''I have something now that I can give everybody.''

Lincoln was not too ill to read in the newspapers accounts of the Gettysburg ceremony. Most of the writers thought the President had delivered a trivial speech. It was some time before the public awoke to the fact that Lincoln's Gettysburg Address was a masterpiece. The nation would remember this speech, which ended with ''. . . that we here highly resolve that these dead shall not have died in vain; that this nation, under God, shall have a new birth of freedom; and that government of the people, by the people, and for the people, shall not perish from the earth.''

The war went on, and the tide was turning now against the South. Lincoln received word that the blockade prevented supplies from reaching the Confederacy, that their soldiers were bare-

Four score and seven years ago our fathers brought forth upon this continent, a new nation, conceived in Liberty, and dedicated to the proposition that all men are created equal.

Now we are engaged in a great civil war, testing whether that nation, or any nation so conceived, and so dedicated, can long endure. We are met on a great battle-field of that war. We have come to dedicate a portion of that field, as a final resting place for those who here gave their lives, that that nation might live. It is altogether fitting and proper that we should do this.

But, in a larger sense, we can not dedicate— we can not consecrate— we can not hallow— this ground. The brave men, living and dead, who struggled here, have consecrated it, far above our poor power to add or detract. The world will little note, nor long remember, what we say here, but it can never forget what they did here. It is for us the living, rather, to be dedicated here to the unfinished work which they who fought here, have, thus far, so nobly advanced. It is rather for us to be here dedicated to the great task remaining before us— that from these honored dead we take increased devotion to that cause for which they here gave the last full measure of devotion— that we here highly resolve that these dead shall not have died in vain— that this nation, under God, shall have a new birth of freedom— and that, government of the people, by the people, for the people, shall not perish from the earth.

Lincoln wrote out six copies of his Gettysburg Address, one of the shortest and most moving speeches by any president.

111

foot and hungry, and that shortages of military supplies crippled Lee's army. The Union army outnumbered the Confederates two to one. Grant and Sherman were tough leaders, with one objective, to win the war.

In this objective they were completely supported by the President. People in the North had forgotten that they had not liked Grant, for he was winning victories, and after the battle of Chattanooga he was called a hero. In February, 1864, Congress revived the rank of Lieutenant General and, with the approval of the public, Lincoln appointed Grant to this post.

Grant took over the command of the Eastern forces and prepared his plan of operations from his camp with the Army of the Potomac. He said to General Meade, "Wherever Lee goes, you will go also." Grant's plan had Lincoln's approval, and Lincoln told the general that he would leave the operations in his hands. News reports to Lincoln were not always good, however, for Lee, with his men few in number as compared with opposing forces, parried Grant's tactics and refused open battle. Instead, Lee lured the armies into the Wilderness again. Lincoln was told that Grant began the siege of Richmond by snapping out, "I propose to fight it out on this line if it takes all summer."

It took more than the summer. In July a daring Confederate raiding party under Jubal Early dashed to the outskirts of Washington and almost penetrated the city. As reinforcements arrived for defense, Lincoln climbed to the top of a building and stood there, watching, paying no attention to bullets hitting close by. He was finally persuaded to leave, for his tall frame made him a target.

Then he went to the crowded hospitals, to walk slowly between rows of cots, smiling and talking, saying to the wounded men, "You must get well."

It seemed to all of the weary people, as well as to Lincoln, that the war would never end. That was a discouraging summer. In the fall news came that General Sherman was breaking into Georgia. He pushed the Confederate forces back to Atlanta and, in December, just outside of the city, fought an important battle. Both sides had heavy casualties, since the Federal army lost over nine thousand, and the Confederates more than ten thousand. Sherman ordered the civilians to leave Atlanta, so that he would not have to deal with a hostile population. To General Halleck he wrote, "If the people raise a howl against my barbarity and cruelty I will answer that war is war, and not popularity-seeking."

From Atlanta Sherman marched his victorious army down through Georgia to Savannah at the sea, and then up to Virginia. They had orders to devastate a strip of territory sixty miles wide as they went—burning, and destroying everything that they did not take. Behind Sherman's army came a wild horde of men called "bummers," who ravaged the countryside to steal whatever they could find both for themselves and to provide supplies for the army, since Sherman had cut off his own food supply and was living on the country.

Lincoln, a humanitarian in his views, and kindly in his personal relationships with people, welcomed the campaign and made no objection to this treatment of civilians. To end the war was his objective. Nothing else was so important to him, although he had to think of the coming election also. As the end of his term of office approached in 1864, Lincoln was doubtful about his re-election. In the North it was difficult to know just what people really did think of him, for lies were told, and printed, and all kinds of stories circulated. Some thought him weak, some called him evil, and some spoke as if he were a saint.

When Congress in 1864 passed a bill that was meant to impose harsh conditions on a defeated

South, Lincoln neither approved nor vetoed it. This brought such violent attacks on him again from extreme radicals that he was inclined to think he would go out of office for good.

His own plans for reconstruction in the South offered general amnesty to Southern officers and soldiers if they surrendered. In a proclamation he had made public in 1863 he had offered full pardon to those who would take an oath to the Constitution and would swear to support the Emancipation Proclamation and all congressional acts that dealt with slavery. Lincoln did not believe in threats, or wish for revenge or reprisals.

In November the election settled the question as to whether the people approved his policies. He was re-elected for a second term as President. As Abraham Lincoln stood up before the crowd in Washington, and once again took the oath of office, there was a deep silence. The nation was still in its greatest struggle, and the wounds of conflict were deep. The President ended his second inaugural address with an appeal for understanding, tolerance, and firmness:

> With malice towards none; with charity for all; with firmness in the right, as God gives us to see the right, let us strive on to finish the work we are in; to bind up the nation's wounds; to care for him who shall have borne the battle, and for his widow

In his second Inaugural Address, on March 4, 1865, Lincoln called on the nation to bind up its wounds and work for peace "with malice toward none; with charity for all."

and his orphans, to do all which may achieve and cherish a just and lasting peace, among ourselves, and with all nations.

As spring once again touched the city of Washington with soft blooms and a southern breeze, the President, with Tad, Mrs. Lincoln, and Mrs. Grant, went on board the *River Queen* to visit General Grant in Virginia at the army headquarters. When they returned they had hopes that at last the war was nearly over. The Confederate army was exhausted, starving, and without supplies. General Lee could not continue to fight. The surrender took place at Appomattox and on that day, April 9, 1865, Lincoln received a telegram from General Grant telling him of the end of the war.

Two days later Lincoln went out on the White House balcony with Tad to speak to a crowd gathered there. After the speech someone asked the President, "What shall we do with the rebels?"

"Hang them!" roared somebody in the crowd. But Tad cried out, "Not hang them. Hang on to them!"

Lincoln's eyes lit up with a smile as he said, "That's it, Tad. You have got it. We must hang on to them."

The President approved of the terms Grant offered to Lee, allowing the Confederate soldiers any horses or mules that they then had, and letting them keep their side arms to return to their homes in peace so long as they observed the laws. Many people in the North felt cheated of revenge, and there was a great outcry against such "weakness."

The world seemed bright and green in the spring after the war ended. The President's face was less tense, softening the tight lines etched deeply there. That "tired spot that could not be got at," as he put it, was resting.

One quiet evening, as Lincoln and his wife talked with friends, he spoke thoughtfully of a dream that he had had recently. When asked about it he said, reluctantly, that he should not have mentioned it—for it was only a dream. He had felt as if he had wakened in the night to hear people crying, and he knew that they were grieving for him. This brought a terrified look to his nervous wife's eyes, so Lincoln changed the subject. His friends glanced at each other, for they could see that the President was in one of his melancholy moods.

On the sunny afternoon of Good Friday, April 14, President and Mrs. Lincoln took a pleasant drive through the city. Mary Lincoln's nervous condition had grown more severe in these years of war and personal sorrow, but on this day she seemed calmer and her sharp tongue was softer than usual. Lincoln talked of going back to Springfield when his term of office was over, back to his law practice. ''I never felt so happy,'' he said.

That night they drove to Ford's Theater to see a play. As he got down from his carriage, Lincoln glanced upward and saw that clouds were scudding across the moon. The President's small party was seated in a box draped with red velvet curtains, and decorated with flags. As the audience cheered, President and Mrs. Lincoln bowed and smiled.

The third act of the play had begun, when suddenly an actor named John Wilkes Booth darted into the unguarded box. Before anyone could move the man drew a pistol and fired at the President. The actor ran to the edge of the box, leaped over the railing to the stage, and ran out through the wings. The stunned crowd was silent until the meaning of this had become clear, and then arose screaming.

President Lincoln was carried across the street to a house. He died there the next morning. As the funeral train moved slowly westward, people stood quietly at railroad stations to pay their respects. The country mourned for Abraham Lincoln, even as he had dreamed. He was buried in

President Lincoln's box at Ford's Theater, photographed shortly after his assassination in April 1865.

Springfield—in the city that had been his home for many years—in the prairie land where, not far away, the slow Sangamon River curved around the deserted village of New Salem.

Lincoln had preserved the nation, and upheld the laws, and he had freed slaves brought to its shores in bondage. People said many things about him, and stories were invented, and legends created until it became hard to tell which were true and which were not. They said he was sad, and funny. He was kind, and thoughtful—and ugly, and somehow noble. They said he was a slow-moving kind of a man.

In the South he was called an abolitionist—a radical who had taken the nation into war, and caused the Southland to be devastated. And in the North some still condemned him as a weak man who would not be hard enough on rebels. Although he was more talked about than any other man, still, for a long time he did not seem real, but only a figure that represented many contradictory things.

When time had passed and the tragic wounds of civil war had healed, Americans came to call Abraham Lincoln a pioneer spirit—a man who expressed the democratic ideals of a plain people. He became known as the Great Emancipator. Just as time has brought to the North admiration for the character and the military genius of Robert E. Lee, so to the South the years have brought a better understanding of the greatness of Abraham Lincoln. To the world he embodies the spirit of freedom, and of the democracy that was meant to be of the people, by the people, and for the people.

AS IN THE HEARTS OF THE PEOPLE
FOR WHOM HE SAVED THE UNION
THE MEMORY OF ABRAHAM LINCOLN
IS ENSHRINED FOREVER

The Lincoln Memorial was dedicated in Washington, D.C., on May 30, 1922. It attracts millions of visitors every year.

For Further Reading

Bruns, Roger. *Abraham Lincoln, U.S. President*. New York: Chelsea House, 1986.

Freedman, Russell. *Lincoln: A Photobiography*. Boston: Houghton Mifflin, 1987.

Metzger, Milton. *Abraham Lincoln*. New York: Franklin Watts, 1987.

Index